Immigration to the United States

Greek
Immigrants

W. Scott Ingram

Robert Asher, Ph.D., General Editor

☑®
Facts On File, Inc.

Immigration to the United States: Greek Immigrants

Facts On File, Inc.
132 West 31st Street
New York NY 10001

Library of Congress Cataloging-in-Publication Data

Ingram, Scott.
  Greek immigrants / W. Scott Ingram.
    p. cm. – (Immigration to the United States)
  Includes bibliographical references and index.
  ISBN 0-8160-5689-7
  1. Greek Americans–History–Juvenile literature. 2. Immigrants–United States–
History–Juvenile literature. 3. Greek Americans–Juvenile literature. I. Title. II. Series.
  E184.G7I54 2004
  304.8'730495–dc22

                                                                                    2004014298

Facts On File books are available at special discounts when purchased in bulk quantities for businesses, associations, institutions, or sales promotions. Please call our Special Sales Department in New York at (212) 967-8800 or (800) 322-8755.

You can find Facts On File on the World Wide Web at http://www.factsonfile.com

Cover design by Cathy Rincon
A Creative Media Applications Production
Interior design: Fabia Wargin & Luís Leon
Editor: Laura Walsh
Copy editor: Laurie Lieb
Proofreader: Tania Bissell
Photo researcher: Jennifer Bright

Photo Credits:
p. 1 © Hulton-Deutsch Collection/CORBIS; p. 4 © Getty Images/Hulton Archive; p. 11 © Getty Images/Hulton Archive; p. 13 © Araldo de Luca/CORBIS; p. 16 © Stefano Bianchetti/CORBIS; p. 22 © Roger Wood/CORBIS; p. 27 © Bettmann/CORBIS; p. 33 © Getty Images/Hulton Archive; p. 36 © Getty Images/Hulton Archive; p. 41 © Getty Images/Hulton Archive; p. 45 © Corbis; p. 46 © Getty Images/Hulton Archive; p. 51 © CORBIS; p. 53 © CORBIS; p. 57 © Getty Images/Hulton Archive; p. 60 © Getty Images/Hulton Archive; p. 65 © AP Photo/Jennifer Szymaszek; p. 67 © AP Photo; p. 70 © Bettmann/CORBIS; p. 73 © AP Photo; p. 74 © James L. Amos/CORBIS; p. 77 © Paul A. Souders/CORBIS; p. 80 © Bettmann/CORBIS; p. 83 © AP Photo/Keith Shimada; p. 87 © AP Photo/ John-Marshall Mantel; p. 90 © Roger Wood/CORBIS; p. 90 © Getty Images/Hulton Archive; p. 90 © Getty Images/Hulton Archive; p. 91 © AP Photo; p. 91 © Paul A. Souders/CORBIS; p. 91 © Getty Images/Hulton Archive

Printed in the United States of America

VH PKG 10 9 8 7 6 5 4 3 2 1

This book is printed on acid-free paper.

Previous page: Newly arrived refugee families pose for a picture after leaving the ship that brought them from Greece in 1922.

Contents

Preface to the Series

A Nation
of Immigrants

Robert Asher, Ph.D.

Human beings have always moved from one place to another. Sometimes they have sought territory with more food or better economic conditions. Sometimes they have moved to escape poverty or been forced to flee from invaders who have taken over their territory. When people leave one country or region to settle in another, their movement is called emigration. When people come into a new country or region to settle, it is called immigration. The new arrivals are called immigrants.

People move from their home country to settle in a new land for two underlying reasons. The first reason is that negative conditions in their native land push them to leave. These are called "push factors." People are pushed to emigrate from their native land or region by such things as poverty, religious persecution, or political oppression.

The second reason that people emigrate is that positive conditions in the new country pull them to the new land. These are called "pull factors." People immigrate to new countries seeking opportunities that do not exist in their native country. Push and pull factors often work together. People leave poor conditions in one country seeking better conditions in another.

Sometimes people are forced to flee their homeland because of extreme hardship, war, or oppression. These immigrants to new lands are called refugees. During times of war or famine, large groups of refugees may immigrate to new countries in

search of better conditions. Refugees have been on the move
from the earliest recorded history. Even today, groups of
refugees are forced to move from one country to another.

Pulled to America

For hundreds of years, people have been pulled to America
seeking freedom and economic opportunity. America has
always been a land of immigrants. The original settlers of
America emigrated from Asia thousands of years ago. These first
Americans were probably following animal herds in search of
better hunting grounds. They migrated to America across a land
bridge that connected the west coast of North America with
Asia. As time passed, they spread throughout North and South
America and established complex societies and cultures.

Beginning in the 1500s, a new group of immigrants came
to America from Europe. The first European immigrants to
America were volunteer sailors and soldiers who were promised
rewards for their labor. Once settlements were established, small
numbers of immigrants from Spain, Portugal, France, Holland,
and England began to arrive. Some were rich, but most were
poor. Most of these emigrants had to pay for the expensive
ocean voyage from Europe to the Western Hemisphere by
promising to work for four to seven years. They were called
indentured servants. These emigrants were pushed out of
Europe by religious persecution, high land prices, and poverty.
They were pulled to America by reports of cheap, fertile land
and by the promise of more religious freedom than they had in
their homelands.

Many immigrants who arrived in America, however, did
not come by choice. Convicts were forcibly transported from
England to work in the American colonies. In addition,

thousands of African men, women, and children were kidnapped in Africa and forced onto slave ships. They were transported to America and forced to work for European masters. While voluntary emigrants had some choice of which territory they would move to, involuntary immigrants had no choice at all. Slaves were forced to immigrate to America from the 1500s until about 1840. For voluntary immigrants, two things influenced where they settled once they arrived in the United States. First, immigrants usually settled where there were jobs. Second, they often settled in the same places as immigrants who had come before them, especially those who were relatives or who had come from the same village or town in their homeland. This is called chain migration. Immigrants felt more comfortable living among people whose language they understood and whom they might have known in the "old country."

Immigrants often came to America with particular skills that they had learned in their native countries. These included occupations such as carpentry, butchering, jewelry making, metal machining, and farming. Immigrants settled in places where they could find jobs using these skills.

In addition to skills, immigrant groups brought their languages, religions, and customs with them to the new land. Each of these many cultures has made unique contributions to American life. Each group has added to the multicultural society that is America today.

Waves of Immigration

Many immigrant groups came to America in waves. In the early 1800s, economic conditions in Europe were growing harsh. Famine in Ireland led to a massive push of emigration of Irish men and women to the United States. A similar number of

German farmers and urban workers migrated to America. They were attracted by high wages, a growing number of jobs, and low land prices. Starting in 1880, huge numbers of people in southern and eastern Europe, including Italians, Russians, Poles, and Greeks, were facing rising populations and poor economies. To escape these conditions, they chose to immigrate to the United States. In the first 10 years of the 20th century, immigration from Europe was in the millions each year, with a peak of 8 million immigrants in 1910. In the 1930s, thousands of Jewish immigrants fled religious persecution in Nazi Germany and came to America.

Becoming a Legal Immigrant

There were few limits on the number of immigrants that could come to America until 1924. That year, Congress limited immigration to the United States to only 100,000 per year. In 1965, the number of immigrants allowed into the United States each year was raised from 100,000 to 290,000. In 1986, Congress further relaxed immigration rules, especially for immigrants from Cuba and Haiti. The new law allowed 1.5 million legal immigrants to enter the United States in 1990. Since then, more than half a million people have legally immigrated to the United States each year.

Not everyone who wants to immigrate to the United States is allowed to do so. The number of people from other countries who may immigrate to America is determined by a federal law called the Immigration and Naturalization Act (INA). This law was first passed in 1952. It has been amended (changed) many times since then.

Following the terrorist attacks on the World Trade Center in New York City and the Pentagon in Washington, D.C., in 2001, Congress made significant changes in the INA. One important change was to make the agency that administers laws concerning immigrants and other people entering the United States part of the Department of Homeland Security (DHS). The DHS is responsible for protecting the United States from attacks by terrorists. The new immigration agency is called the Citizenship and Immigration Service (CIS). It replaced the previous agency, which was called the Immigration and Naturalization Service (INS).

When noncitizens enter the United States, they must obtain official permission from the government to stay in the country. This permission is called a visa. Visas are issued by the CIS for a specific time period. In order to remain in the country permanently, an immigrant must obtain a permanent resident visa, also called a green card. This document allows a person to live, work, and study in the United States for an unlimited amount of time.

To qualify for a green card, an immigrant must have a sponsor. In most cases, a sponsor is a member of the immigrant's family who is a U.S. citizen or holds a green card. The government sets an annual limit of 226,000 on the number of family members who may be sponsored for permanent residence. In addition, no more than 25,650 immigrants may come from any one country.

In addition to family members, there are two other main avenues to obtaining a green card. A person may be sponsored by a U.S. employer or may enter the Green Card Lottery. An employer may sponsor a person who has unique work qualifications. The Green Card Lottery randomly selects 50,000 winners each year to receive green cards. Applicants for the lottery may be from any country from which immigration is allowed by U.S. law.

However, a green card does not grant an immigrant U.S. citizenship. Many immigrants have chosen to become citizens of the United States. Legal immigrants who have lived in the United States for at least five years and who meet other requirements may apply to become naturalized citizens. Once these immigrants qualify for citizenship, they become full-fledged citizens and have all the rights, privileges, and obligations of other U.S. citizens.

Even with these newer laws, there are always more people who want to immigrate to the United States than are allowed by law. As a result, some people choose to come to the United States illegally. Illegal immigrants do not have permission from the U.S. government to enter the country. Since 1980, the number of illegal immigrants entering the United States, especially from Central and South America, has increased greatly. These illegal immigrants are pushed by poverty in their homelands and pulled by the hope of a better life in the United States. Illegal immigration cannot be exactly measured, but it is believed that between 1 million and 3 million illegal immigrants enter the United States each year.

This series, Immigration to the United States, describes the history of the immigrant groups that have come to the United States. Some came because of the pull of America and the hope of a better life. Others were pushed out of their homelands. Still others were forced to immigrate as slaves. Whatever the reasons for their arrival, each group has a unique story and has made a unique contribution to the American way of life.

Right: This photo from about 1890 shows four priests of the Greek Orthodox or Eastern Church wearing their traditional robes and hats.

Introduction

Greek Immigration

Becoming Greek Americans

Among the many groups that immigrated to the United States in the late 18th and early 19th centuries, one ethnic group that arrived with a deep sense of its own ancient heritage was the Greeks. The Greeks were descended from a culture that many considered the foundation of Western civilization. They were among the millions of immigrants from southern and eastern Europe that arrived in the United States between 1880 and 1920. During that 40 year period, more than 600,000 Greeks came to the United States.

As fiercely proud as most Greeks were of their ancient heritage, the modern nation of Greece was a relatively young. For centuries, the Greek peninsula had been under the iron rule of the Ottoman Empire of Turkey. Only after a revolt in 1821 did the Ottoman rulers grant independence to the modern nation of Greece. By that time, many Greeks had left their original homeland and scattered across Turkey as well as the Balkan Peninsula in southern Europe. In fact, during the great period of immigration, more Greeks lived outside of Greece than in it.

From 1890 to 1900, the first decade of major Greek immigration, more than 90 percent of all Greek immigrants were men. Most of them came to America to earn money to support their families. More than half of all these Greek immigrants returned to Greece during the last decade of the 19th century.

Whether they came from Greece, Turkey, or elsewhere, almost all Greeks who came to America settled in urban areas. Greek immigrant communities were located mainly in the manufacturing cities of the northern United States between New York City and Chicago, Illinois.

Although many Greek immigrants to the United States shared pride in their heritage, this sense of "Greekness" was not based on coming from a certain nation. The main unifying force for Greek immigrants was the Greek Orthodox Church, which is a branch of Christianity distinctly different from the Catholic church and Protestantism.

In some ways, the immigration and assimilation of Greek Americans into the United States resemble the experience of other immigrant groups from the same era and region. In other ways, their immigration experience was unique. No matter what obstacles they faced, Greek Americans saw a connection between themselves and their new country and believed they could succeed in a land with a tradition partly based on Greek culture.

Most Greek Americans know that they are a blend of two cultures, one traditionally Greek and one firmly established in the United States. 🔳

Opposite: *This detail shows Alexander the Great in an ancient Roman mosaic.*

Chapter One

Ancient People, New Nation

Greece and Western Civilization

Greek Beginnings

Greek Americans are the descendants of one of the great cultures of the ancient world. Centuries before the Roman Empire and the Christian era, the rocky, mountainous Peloponnesian Peninsula and surrounding islands in the Aegean Sea were home to one of the world's great civilizations. Located southeast of the "boot heel" of Italy in the eastern end of the Mediterranean Sea, reaching toward the Middle East, that civilization is known today as the Greek Empire (330 B.C.–146 B.C.). The empire itself, however, was not a single nation. Instead, it was a collection of what were known as city-states, each operating under a different government. Some of the city-states were Athens, Sparta, Thessaly, and Macedonia. Over the centuries, these city-states came to be thought of as a single empire.

Greece

Although the great achievements of the Greek Empire are still studied today, no nation called Greece ever existed in the ancient world. In fact, at certain times, the city-states were at war with each other. At other times, they joined forces to fight invaders. At no time, however, was there a central Greek government or a capital city of the empire, as Rome was for the Roman Empire. The Roman Empire conquered the city-states of Greece as it rose to power. After that conquest in the first century B.C., the Greek city-states became cities in the vast region controlled by Rome. This area included most of Europe, much of the Middle East, and the coast of North Africa.

Although Rome conquered the Greeks, the influence of Greeks continued to be felt in the ancient world. Greek was the main language spoken throughout the Mediterranean region. Greek gods were adopted by Romans, although their names were changed. For example, Zeus, the most powerful god in Greek mythology, became Jove to the Romans.

Thousands of years after its glory days, ancient Greek culture is still notable for producing some of history's most famous politicians, scientists, writers, and military leaders. Democracy, the foundation of the U.S. government, was first practiced in the ancient Greek city of Athens. The word *democracy* itself comes from a Greek word meaning "rule of the people." One of the first great democratically elected leaders was Pericles, the leader of Athens.

In the sciences, the Greek mathematician Euclid created geometry. The scientist Ptolemy created some of the first astronomical charts of the skies. Literature too was important to the Greeks. The poet Homer, born on the island of Chios, wrote the *Odyssey* and the *Iliad*, works that are still studied in many American schools. This society also produced one of history's most successful military leaders, Alexander the Great, who conquered much of Asia while he was in his early twenties.

Aesop's Fables

One of the most well-known Greek storytellers was a slave born in 599 B.C. He entertained his master with stories about animals that had human personalities. Each story had a moral, an important lesson.

The slave's stories were so entertaining that his grateful master granted him his freedom. The storyteller's name was Aesop. Today, Aesop's fables are known to millions. Among them are "The Tortoise and the Hare," "The City Mouse and the Country Mouse," and "The Wolf in Sheep's Clothing."

In the first century A.D., the Greek peninsula became one of the first regions outside of the Middle East to convert to Christianity. What became known as the Greek or Eastern Orthodox Church was one of the earliest organized forms of the Christian religion. Missionaries from the Greek church carried the faith north to the Balkan Peninsula into the nation now known as Serbia and eastward into the nation that became known as Russia.

Between A.D. 100 and A.D. 1400, the Greek Orthodox Church and the Catholic Church were the two main branches of Christianity. Although the city-states of Greece were still separate kingdoms, the Greek Orthodox faith eventually became a unifying force for the people of the region that included the Balkan Peninsula, the Peloponnesian Peninsula, and the country of Turkey, northeast of Greece on the coast of the Aegean Sea.

In the 15th century, the major city in that region was Constantinople. Located in Turkey, for centuries the city had been the capital of the Eastern Roman Empire, as well as the center of the Eastern Orthodox faith. In 1453, Constantinople was conquered by Sultan Mehmed II, the leader of a group of Muslims known as the Ottoman Turks.

The Ottoman Empire became one of the most powerful empires of that time. Within two years after the fall of Constantinople, the Greek peninsula, the Aegean islands, and much of the Middle East were controlled by the Ottoman Empire. For the next 350 years, Greece was part of the Ottoman Empire. The Ottomans changed the name of Constantinople to the name by which it is known today, Istanbul.

At the height of its power, the Ottoman Empire ruled much of eastern Europe and the Middle East, an area nearly as large as that of the Roman Empire. While Muslims received favored treatment under law, Ottoman rulers allowed their non-Muslim subjects—Jewish, Catholic, and Greek Orthodox—to practice their own religions. This helped the rulers govern a wide area.

Under this arrangement, the leader of the Greek Orthodox Church, called the patriarch, became a powerful political leader. As a result, the Greek Orthodox Church itself played a critical role in the development of what came to be considered "Greek" society before there was even a nation known as Greece. In its role, the church kept the Greek language alive, and its religious schools carried on the traditions of Greek culture. Because the church's power was dependent on the approval of the Ottoman rulers, however, the church became very conservative. For example, it ignored the independent and democratic traditions of ancient Greece city-states. Instead it demanded complete obedience to religious laws. Nevertheless, the patriarchs had enormous influence.

The Greek Dispersion

Like the Roman Empire before it, the Ottoman Empire was so large that previous local, national, and regional boundaries were forgotten. People under Ottoman rule were free to move about the empire. Over the centuries of Ottoman rule, many Greeks chose to leave their traditional homeland to seek freedom and opportunity elsewhere. Greeks moved in large numbers north into the Balkan Peninsula and east to Romania. Greeks also settled in coastal cities along the Black Sea and the Mediterranean Sea in Turkey. Many of the most successful merchants and traders based in Istanbul were actually ethnic Greeks.

Many Greeks also chose to flee the rule of the Ottoman Turks. In the 16th and 17th centuries, Greek communities arose outside the Ottoman Empire. Hundreds of thousands of Greeks, for example, moved into the countries today known as Austria and Hungary. Many thousands more settled in Russia, which shared a religious heritage with the Greeks.

Because of their strong traditions of sea exploration, many Greeks who emigrated from their homeland also became merchants and traders like the Greeks in Turkey. In fact, much of the trade that developed between the Ottoman Empire and other Mediterranean regions was done by Greeks, who became a link between the various regions. As world exploration increased during the 16th and 17th centuries, Greek merchants and traders established communities along the Mediterranean coast in Venice, Livorno, Naples (in present-day Italy), and Marseille (in present-day France). Other European port cities such as Amsterdam (the Netherlands), Antwerp (Belgium), London, Liverpool (England), and Paris (France) also had large Greek populations.

Greek Sailors

The early Europeans who sailed to the American continent were well aware of the sailing skills of the Greeks. Greek sailors with names such as Theodoros and Petros the Cretan were enlisted in the crews of Ferdinand Magellan and other Spanish explorers. Christopher Columbus sailed to the Greek island of Chios to recruit sailors for his exploration as well. Among those he recruited was a Greek named John Griego, who sailed with Columbus on his first voyage.

Perhaps the most famous Greek sailor was Apostolos Valerianos. Known in history books as Juan de Fuca, he was the first European to sail the narrow, island-filled waters separating Washington State from British Columbia, Canada. The Strait of Juan de Fuca in Puget Sound bear his name.

Along with the Greek Orthodox Church, the dispersed Greek communities also helped to develop the idea of what it meant to be "Greek." In their homeland, most Greeks felt a loyalty to their extended family and friends or to their place of origin. Among Greek emigrants living in foreign countries far away from their homeland, the idea of a Greek nation gained popularity.

By the late 1700s, the support for the formation of a Greek nation was strong among Greeks in Europe and elsewhere outside the Ottoman Empire. This desire for an independent homeland increased as news of the American Revolution (1775–1783) spread around the world. Greeks felt a great deal of pride knowing that many of the principles stated in the Declaration of Independence and the U.S. Constitution had been first written down in ancient Greek city-states. The creation of a democratic government based on these concepts had enormous power for Greeks. They had come to hate the Ottoman rule as much as Americans hated being controlled by the British.

Greek Constitutions

The democratic principles that the U.S. Constitution was based on were first written down in ancient Greece. Since the Greek city-state of Athens was known to have practiced democracy, it was long believed that the constitution of Athens was the first such written document in world history. However, a section of what appears to be the oldest known written constitution in the world was found on the Greek island of Chios in 1907. It was determined that this constitution was inscribed about 2,600 years ago on four sides of a stone block about 2 feet (0.6 m) high and more than 1 foot (0.3 m) wide. Since the island of Chios was under Turkish rule when the

"Constitution Stone" was discovered in 1907, the stone was sent to the Archeological Museum at Istanbul, Turkey, where it remains today.

The ancient constitution describes a system of government that resembled that of the United States. For example, there were three branches of government. The executive leader was called the *Basileus*. There was also a legislative, or lawmaking, body called the Council of the People. In the judicial branch, legal cases were heard by judges called *Demarchos*. The Constitution Stone also includes laws for punishing and removing from office officials who commit crimes.

The first revolt against Ottoman rule took place in the 1780s, when Greek rebels from Russia secretly entered the Peloponnesian Peninsula to attack Ottoman forces there. The attempt was crushed by the Ottoman forces, but the stage had been set. The failed rebellion caused the Ottoman rulers to become increasingly brutal in their treatment of the Greeks. This treatment, in turn, increased the widespread hatred of the Ottoman Empire by all Greeks.

By 1820, the hatred had reached the point of revolution both within the Greek homeland and outside its traditional borders. At that time, thousands of people in the Balkan and

Peloponnesian peninsulas had died in a famine. The Ottoman rulers had done nothing to end the mass starvation and the people were prepared to revolt. Meanwhile, Greek emigrants had organized secret armies in several cities across Europe. These groups, made up of men from all levels of Greek society, were united in their desire to drive the Ottoman rulers from the Greek peninsula.

In 1821, the war against the Ottoman Empire began. The conflict, known as the Greek War of Independence, was the first national revolution against a foreign rule since the American Revolution. The bloody conflict against the most powerful Muslim empire of the time dragged on for more than 10 years. Destruction was widespread, and thousands of civilians were killed. One of the worst such episodes took place on the island of Chios, which the Turkish forces invaded in 1822. More than 25,000 civilians were massacred and almost 50,000 were taken as slaves.

As news of the Chios massacre spread, it created widespread support for Greek independence across Europe and the United States. Some Americans, as well as European volunteers, traveled to Greece to join the war against the Ottoman Turks. The English poet Lord Byron was among the many non-Greek volunteers killed in the Greek War of Independence.

It's a Fact!

The Greek Revolution began during the U.S. presidency of James Monroe. In a message to Congress on December 3, 1822, Monroe expressed his "strong hope" that Greece would gain its independence. This led to a period in early U.S. history known as "Greek Fever." Over the decade of the Greek War of Independence, dozens of towns in several states took Greek names. The towns of Athens and Macedonia in Ohio were named at that time. Ypsilanti, Michigan, was also founded then. Ithaca, New York, also took a Greek name, and a small village in upstate New York changed its name to "Greece."

The ruins of the Acropolis in Athens are perched on a hill overlooking the ancient city.

Among the Americans who helped the cause of Greek independence was Samuel Gridley Howe, who became the chief surgeon in the Greek army. He later led the antislavery movement in the United States. American Nicholas Biddle left his U.S. government position as minister to France to volunteer in Greece. In his memoirs, he wrote:

> *[It is] . . . sad remembrance of what Greece once was . . . The . . . relation between the Greeks and Turks is that of slave to master. The Turks pay no taxes; the whole burden falls upon the Greeks. . . . The Turks always go armed; all kinds of weapons are forbidden to the Greeks. A Turk takes . . . from*

the peasants whatever he may want. . . . Such . . . is the alarm
which their very name inspires, that it is the practice . . . to
pacify children . . . by saying there is a Turk coming.

As the war continued, the leaders of the north African nation
of Egypt offered to assist their fellow Muslims, the Ottoman
Turks. This drew a response from European powers such as France,
Great Britain, Russia, and several German kingdoms. These
Western powers feared that such an alliance would bring the
eastern Mediterranean region under Muslim control. During the
late 1820s, Greece was in danger of serving as the battleground for
a world war similar to the conflict, World War I, that would start a
century later in the Balkan Peninsula to the north.

Finally, in 1832, Ottoman rulers, exhausted by a decade of
war, signed an agreement creating the first independent nation
of Greece. Ironically, British, French, German, and Russian
forces rushed into the war-torn area as the Ottoman forces with-
drew. Rulers of these Western nations explained that their presence was to protect the Greek people. Nevertheless, the
Europeans declared that they had the right to define the borders
of Greece and to create a system of government for the new
nation. Instead of a democracy based on the United States,
however, the new Greece became a monarchy similar to those of
Europe. The Europeans also put Greece's first ruler on the
throne. He was a seventeen-year-old German prince named
Otto, who was a Roman Catholic.

In the end, the nation of Greece was nothing like the "new
empire" of which many Greeks had dreamed for years. Instead, it
was a weak, foreign-dominated country, ruined by war. While
many westerners had helped in the revolution, the rulers of
European kingdoms had no intention of allowing a democracy
to arise in Greece. Greece was deeply in debt to the larger powers,
and its people were too weak to resist the armies of western
Europe after 10 years of war. Thus, they were forced to accept

a monarchy, the form of government that controlled most of the nations of the world. Ironically, after a 10-year fight for freedom, Greece was ruled by an appointed king who followed a faith different from the faith of the Greek people. Nevertheless, for the first time in history, Greece was a nation. Greeks in the country and outside its borders experienced a strong sense of national pride.

Saint Nicholas

The original Santa Claus, Saint Nicholas, was a Greek born in Turkey in the fourth century. He was very religious from an early age and devoted his life to Christianity. Nicholas became widely known for his generosity to the poor and his love of children. In Greece, Saint Nicholas is the patron saint who protects sailors. According to Greek tradition, his clothes are drenched with brine (salty water) and his beard drips with seawater because he fights the waves to reach sinking ships and rescue them from the angry sea.

The legend of Saint Nicholas as a generous man who loved children was kept alive by the Dutch. In Holland at Christmas, Dutch children placed their wooden shoes by the fireplace in hopes that they would be filled with treats. Early Dutch settlers in New York spelled the name of this special person "Sinterklaas," which eventually became "Santa Claus."

Difficult Decades

The early years of the new Greek nation were extremely difficult. Most villages and cities lay in ruins. Agriculture, the most important part of the economy, had been destroyed by the war. More than half of the nation's olive trees, vineyards, and flour mills had been destroyed. More than 90 percent of its live-stock had been killed.

The people of Greece turned to the new king, and the nations that put him in power, for help. Because agriculture was the key to the nation's economic health, land and money were loaned to farmers. As soon as word spread that such help was available, however, other people requested assistance. Military leaders who had led the rebel forces demanded land and local political power as their reward for victory. Merchant ship owners demanded to be repaid for losses in naval battles. Soldiers wanted the pay that was owed to them, as well as rewards of land.

Despite economic support from European powers, it was impossible for the new government to meet all of the demands placed on it. Within a decade, a new type of government, a constitutional monarchy, replaced the absolute monarchy of Otto. Under the new government, the king agreed to share power with a legislative body called a parliament, which was led by a prime minister.

The establishment of a new government gave hope to people who were still struggling to recover from the war and its aftermath. With more Greeks in government, they believed, money and land would be easier to obtain. Yet those hopes proved false. Many of the delegates elected to parliament owed their elections to the political influence of large landholders and other wealthy Greeks.

The new lawmakers used their positions to benefit their supporters by repealing (ending) taxes and granting other political favors. As a result, Greece was soon in a worse economic crisis than the one it had endured in the first years of independence. The only way to pay for the government was to raise taxes on agriculture. This meant that the land and money originally given to peasants after independence was soon taken back from them in the form of taxes.

The corrupt parliamentary system in Greece during the mid-1800s caused economic problems that lasted for most of the 19th century. The nation sank so deeply into debt that it was forced to borrow millions of dollars from foreign powers. By the 1880s, almost half of Greece's annual budget expenses were for repayment of foreign loans. Again and again, the parliament raised taxes on people in the agricultural class. These people had little say in the government. Economic conditions for these lower classes were near disaster. Author Stephos Zotos writes: "There was no progress, or economic development. Greek families did not . . . starve; however, under the constant pressure . . . [they] had little opportunity to acquire the economic assets that bring security and dignity to human beings."

By the 1890s, small farmers had no more to give. They had been taxed to the point that they barely had enough money to feed their families. They had no money to spend on other things, which would have helped Greece's economy.

During that decade, prices fell on agricultural products during a worldwide economic depression. This meant that now the farmers would earn even less when they tried to sell their products. As a result, the economy of Greece collapsed. By 1897, Greece was a bankrupt nation. The government could not pay for the most basic expenses such as salaries and military goods. For many of the poorest Greeks, especially those who farmed the land, there was no choice but to look elsewhere for the money they needed to survive. Few wanted to leave home, but most had no choice. ✵

Opposite: *An extended family joins other Greek immigrants as they disembark on Ellis Island.*

Chapter Two

In Search of a Better Life

Greeks Come to America

The First Great Wave

The first Greek immigrants to the United States arrived during the Greek War of Independence. In fact, the first official record of immigration from Greece to America occurred in 1824, with the arrival of four immigrants from the island of Chios. Following the massacre on Chios in 1822, a number of orphaned boys were placed on board ships bound to the United States.

For the next 50 years, Greeks came to the United States in small numbers. At a time when million of immigrants from other European countries entered the United States, fewer than 2,000 Greek immigrants entered the country. The main reason for the low immigration numbers during this time was that the Greeks, for the first time in 300 years, were citizens of an independent nation. Many Greeks wanted to rebuild their country after the damage caused by Ottoman control.

Many of the early Greek immigrants to the United States chose to come to a seaport city with a warm climate that resembled that of their homeland—New Orleans, Louisiana. New Orleans is the home of the oldest Greek community in the United States. It is also the location of the first Greek Orthodox Church in the United States, which was built in 1866.

The pattern of immigration changed for Greeks, as it did for many eastern Europeans, with the development of steam travel after the American Civil War (1861–1865). By the 1880s, steamships had replaced sailing vessels and had shortened the voyage from eastern Mediterranean ports to New York City from months to weeks.

The first significant wave of Greek immigrants to the United States occurred after 1890. By that time, the Greek economy was in the final stages of collapse. Many immigrants were peasants and poor farmers who had been driven to poverty by government tax and land policies. A significant number of the first wave of Greek immigrants, however, came from areas outside of Greece.

During the last half of the 19th century, in fact, more Greeks lived outside of the country than inside its borders. Warfare and economic conditions had driven many Greeks into the Balkan Peninsula, into Turkey, as far south as Egypt, and to many other locations along the coast of the Mediterranean Sea.

The First Greek Settlement

Although the first Greek immigrants came to the United States in the 1820s, they were not the first Greeks in North America. In 1763, Great Britain gained control of a section of northern Florida. In 1767, Scottish physician Dr. Andrew Turnbull was given land in Florida near present-day Daytona by King George III of Great Britain. Turnbull, whose wife was Greek, called his colony New Smyrna after the Greek city where she had been born. Realizing that British settlers might have difficulty working in the heat and humidity in Florida, Turnbull recruited Greek peasants instead.

In 1768, three ships under Turnbull's control landed at New Smyrna. On board were more than 1,400 Greek men, women, and children. What they found was a swampland with no shelter, alligators, and clouds of disease-carrying mosquitoes. Most of the settlers wanted to return home, but they had signed letters to Turnbull in which they agreed to work for a set number of years. At the end of that time, it was agreed, Turnbull would give them each a small plot of land.

In fact, the Greeks were little more than slaves. Greeks who did not work hard were beaten or chained to heavy iron balls. Some were chained to logs in the fields so they could not run away. Death and disease were everywhere. More than 400 Greeks died in the first year of the colony's existence. In 1776, when the American Revolution began, Turnbull abandoned New Smyrna and returned to Great Britain. The surviving Greeks returned to their homeland and the colony vanished.

Because Greek communities were widely scattered across Europe and Asia, it is difficult to know exactly how many Greeks came to the United States during the 20 years between 1890 and 1910. Social scientists who have researched immigration patterns during that period believe that more than two-thirds of all immigrants from Turkey, for example, were Greeks. Other cities and regions outside of Greece also sent large numbers of Greeks to the United States.

Wherever they came from, almost all Greeks going to the United States left from the port of Naples on the southwest coast of Italy. The ships operating out of this port were generally considered to have the worst traveling conditions of any of the ships crossing the Atlantic Ocean. In 1888, a ticket from Naples to New York City cost about $10, an amount equal to many months' wages in Greece. (This amount is equivalent to about $189 in today's money.) For this price, immigrants were usually confined below decks for most of the trip, a travel class known as steerage. Conditions were dreadful during these trips. An investigative reporter who made the trip from Naples wrote:

> *How can a steerage passenger remember that he is a human being when he must first pick the worms from his food . . . and eat in a stuffy, stinking bunk, or in the hot . . . atmosphere of a compartment where 150 men sleep, or [next] to a seasick man?*

It's a Fact!

Many of the first Greek immigrants to New Orleans came from the island of Chios. These Greeks were widely known for their seafaring skills. While many of the early cities in the United States named their streets after famous Americans, such as Washington, the oldest streets of New Orleans have the names of Greek towns. Among the "Greek" streets in the city are Telemachus Street, Terpsichou Street, and Thalia Street.

Strangers in a New Land

The first Greek immigrants to the United States were almost always male. Records show that between 1890 and 1910, more than 90 percent of all Greek immigrants to the United States were men between the ages of 18 and 35. Most of these immigrants were unmarried. Few planned to remain in the United States longer than was necessary to earn enough money to support their families back home. These young men, some as young as 14, expected to return to Greece. Most hoped to return with enough money to buy land in Greece for their families or provide dowries (wedding payments) for their sisters. Others had individual dreams of earning enough money in the United States to return to Greece to marry, buy land, and start families of their own.

Most of these young men had not broken all ties with their homeland. They came to the United States to earn money, but the opportunity to build a life in a newly independent Greece made them want to return. During the last decades of the 19th century, for example, more than 10,000 Greeks left the United States to return to Greece every year. Between 1908 and 1924, almost half of those who had immigrated to the United States returned to Greece.

The first wave of Greek immigration to the United States in the late 19th and early 20th centuries was just one part of the nearly 20 million people who came from Europe to the United States during that time. Many immigrants came to the United States to escape poverty, war, and ethnic violence. Others sought political freedom and economic opportunity that was unavailable in their homelands.

Whatever their reasons for leaving their homelands, many immigrants were drawn to the United States because of the enormous industrial expansion there. The manufacture of steel used in steamships, and especially railroads, created a steady supply of jobs in mines and factories. Greeks and many other immigrants were also drawn to the United States by stories of high pay and excellent living conditions. These stories were exaggerated. For many immigrants, the reality was disappointing.

Changing Names

Many people believe that when immigrants entered the United States at Ellis Island, their names were changed. The explanation is that when immigrants who spoke little or no English, were asked for their names, they might have given an incorrect reply, which was then written down on official documents. It is also believed that clerks working at Ellis Island misunderstood foreign-sounding immigrant names or found simpler ways to spell them.

In reality, clerks at Ellis Island did not write down names. Instead they worked from passenger lists created by the owners of the ships the immigrants traveled on. If a name was recorded incorrectly, the mistake had likely occurred back in the immigrants' home country, not at Ellis Island.

In general, name changes occurred after immigrants left Ellis Island. Most immigrants came to the United States to work, and there was heavy competition for jobs. Employers often found foreign names difficult to pronounce and preferred workers who seemed more "American." By making their names sound less foreign and more American, immigrants hoped to have a better chance at a job.

For that reason, many Greek immigrants Americanized their names. For example, the name "Eleni" became "Helen," "Iannes" became "John," and "Demetri" became "James." Some Greeks also shortened or changed their last names. For instance, the common Greek suffix -poulos, which means "son of" in Greek, was often dropped. The last name of vice president Spiro Agnew's immigrant father, for example, was Anagnostopoulos.

A group of immigrants sits with their belongings in a railroad
waiting hall on Ellis Island, New York, in 1895.

Even so, many immigrants from northern and western
Europe, especially those who spoke English, felt welcomed in
the United States. Most were able to find work and blend in to
the American culture. On the other hand, Greeks and other
immigrant groups from southern and eastern Europe were
received more coldly. Greeks, in particular, who spoke a
language and used an alphabet unlike anything close to English,
were among the most despised of all immigrant groups.

Like most immigrants from Europe during this period,
Greeks arrived in New York City. There they were detained at
the Immigration Center on Ellis Island in New York Harbor.

Even before the steamships landed, however, American officials boarded the ships. In a 1902 article in a magazine called *The World's Work*, author Edward Lowry describes the process:

> *Inspectors go aboard from the … [navy ships] … and obtain the [passenger list], which the steamship companies must supply. These [lists] must show: Full name–age–sex–whether married or single–calling or occupation–whether able to read or write– nationality–last residence–seaport for landing in the United States–final destination in the United States … the immigrant's condition of health, mentally and physically and whether deformed or crippled; and if so, from what cause. It is a searching census, indeed.*

That was just the first step for immigrants. Many of them were ill, frightened by unfamiliar surroundings, and had no acquaintances to meet them. Lowry describes the next stage:

> *When the steamship reaches her pier the inspectors discharge . . . immigrants . . . unnecessary to examine (usually not over fifteen or twenty). All the others are transferred to barges and taken to Ellis Island. There on the main floor of the big immigration building they are divided into groups according to the lists. Later, in lines set off by iron railings, they undergo "primary inspection." Each immigrant is questioned to see if his answers ally with the lists. If they do, he is discharged; if they do not, he is detained for special inquiry by inspectors, who decide all questionable cases. . . . The immigrants are kept in the big deten- tion room until the railway agents take them to board trains to their [destination].*

In his book, Lowry also describes the different groups that "flooded" New York's Ellis Island. Like many Americans of the time, Lowry had prejudiced attitudes toward ethnic groups.

Once the stream came mainly from the North of Europe: now it comes chiefly from the South—the undesirable countries . . . Roughly speaking, the North-of-Europe people make better citizens than those from the South of Europe. The better class go to the country and the worst to the cities. Greeks are . . . the least desirable of all.

Attitudes such as Lowry's were common. Greeks were often barred from jobs reserved for "whites," that is, immigrants from northern Europe. In many cities, Greeks were to forced to live and eat in segregated (separate) areas. In 1909 a restaurant in a California city posted a sign that read: "Pure American. No Rats. No Greeks." Greek-American sociologist Dan Georgakas writes, "As far as most Americans were concerned, the Greeks were the scum of Europe."

The shock of arrival in a strange, often unfriendly land rapidly created a feeling of homesickness. In 1902, Lowry wrote of the immigrants, many of them Greek, who gathered often in southern Manhattan:

Homesickness drives certain of the foreign born residents of New York to the Battery Park sea wall. . . . On sunny mornings the long rows of benches facing the sea are full of men . . . watching the ships come in. . . . Their talk is of home . . . of the vineyards, of [Greek] villages, and of . . . Mediterranean cities.

Padrones and Patriarchs

Immigration records show that most Greek immigrants were uneducated boys and young men who had left poverty-stricken rural areas. After a journey in the filthy hold of a steamship, they had arrived in a crowded, cold environment.

Because the first Greek immigrants to the United States were mostly young men who planned to return to their homeland, it was rare for any new arrival to be welcomed by relatives already in America. With no one to greet them, it was natural for the newcomers to band together with others who spoke their language. They sought living quarters in the same areas and often worked in the same jobs. These early groups eventually settled into neighborhoods that were called "Greek Towns" in many cities.

Money Carried by Immigrants

Part of the process of accepting immigrants at Ellis Island was determining how much money each person or family was bringing into the United States. At their examination, immigrants were asked to show their money. The money was carefully counted, and, after the amount was recorded, the money was returned.

According to Ellis Island records, in 1901, the average immigrant arrived with slightly more than $14 (about $320 in today's money). Immigrant groups from western Europe were among those who arrived with the most money. For example, French and German immigrants arrived with an average of more than $30 per person. On the other hand, Greek immigrants arrived in the United States with an average of slightly more than $11.

With little money, no education, and few skills, they had to survive in a place where they did not speak the language or know anyone. As a result, many Greek immigrants were forced to turn to what became known among immigrants from southern Europe as the padrone system.

Padrone is an Italian word meaning "protector" or "owner." A padrone was generally an older immigrant who spoke reasonably good English. He was able to find rooms in crowded buildings for immigrants and would provide them with food. Each immigrant group that used the padrone system, such as the Greeks or Italians, had padrones who spoke their own language. In return, the immigrants worked to repay the padrone. Greek immigrants often sold candy, fruit, or flowers on the street to repay their padrones. The youngest Greek immigrants who entered the padrone arrangement were almost always shoeshine boys.

Needless to say, padrones often took advantage of Greek immigrants' ignorance of the English language and of American laws. Instead of earning money to take back to Greece, some immigrants fell into debt and were forced to endure terrible working and living conditions.

While most immigrants had worked on farms in Greece and elsewhere in Europe, few Greeks had the opportunity to work in rural areas in the United States. In general, Greeks settled in coastal cities such as New York and Baltimore, Maryland, as well as in New England industrial areas. They also traveled westward, and for many years, the largest Greek immigrant community in the United States was located in Chicago, Illinois. Some had the experience of working for dishonest bosses in their first jobs as dishwashers, laborers, or street vendors and in the fur and garment industries. After that, many Greek immigrants decided that they would prefer to work for themselves. A large number of Greek Americans during this time opened small businesses such as candy stores and grocery stores.

Many other Greek immigrants opened restaurants. These were not eating places that specialized in Greek foods. Rather, they were small diners that featured inexpensive dishes. These diners had names like "The Athenian" (after the Greek city of Athens) and were usually located in immigrant neighborhoods.

These diners, along with Greek-owned coffeehouses, were the main meeting places for immigrants in "Greek Towns." Small businesses such as these were ideal for immigrants who preferred to work for themselves. These businesses required little money to start. They could use other immigrants as employees. Finally, they served an important need in the poor communities. People who could not afford to eat elsewhere, or who were not welcomed in places where other Americans socialized, were welcomed at the Greek diners.

Not all Greeks, of course, followed this same path. Many Greek workers performed manual labor. By 1907, it is estimated that about 30,000 Greeks had jobs in factories, on construction gangs, and in mines. Many Greek immigrants worked in textile manufacturing, especially in mills in the Northeast such as those in Lowell, Massachusetts.

A group of newsboys and shoeshine boys in caps play dice on a sidewalk in front of a store about 1910.

Other Greeks went west to Nevada, Utah, and California to work in mines and on railroads. The Utah Fuel Company employed thousands of Greeks in coal mines across the state. Greeks laid much of the railroad track that began to crisscross the vast states of Oregon and Washington in the late 19th and early 20th centuries. In the South, a large community of Greeks from the Aegean Islands immigrated to Florida, where they developed fishing and sponge-diving businesses.

Wherever Greek immigrants settled, however, the center of their community was not diners or coffeehouses. It was the Greek Orthodox Church. As it had during the years of Ottoman control in Greece, the church helped Greeks connect with their culture and heritage. Because they were considered "inferior" by the dominant American culture of the time, Greek immigrants had little desire to become "Greek Americans." Instead, they turned to the church for a sense of ethnic pride and community.

Greek immigrants were fortunate that their faith and their national heritage were so closely linked. That was not the case in many other religions that were practiced in America. The Roman Catholic Church, for example, drew immigrants from Ireland, Italy, and France. Even though the Catholic services were held in the ancient language of Latin, each nationality had a different approach to the faith. The Protestant faiths of northern European immigrants were even more varied, with different practices and even different languages.

The Greek Orthodox Church, however, which had developed in Greece, Serbia, and Russia, served a smaller number of people. Few other nations or people had followed the Orthodox faith. It remained unchanged in the lives of many Greeks for more than 1,000 years, no matter where they lived. In a foreign and often unwelcoming environment, the church was a place of comfort for Greeks who had come from Turkey, France, Greece, and many other places. It was a place in which Greeks could share language, faith, and an ethnic pride that was not respected in their day-to-day dealings with other Americans. The church connected Greeks not only to their ancient traditions but to the newly independent homeland that many of them missed.

The establishment of Greek Orthodox churches usually followed a series of steps as the community grew. As more and more Greeks moved into a town or city, they made up a community. The people of these communities contributed funds to establish local churches. Once enough money was raised to construct a building for worship, the community contacted the patriarch in Greece to request that a priest be sent to oversee the religious services.

As communities grew, churches could afford to build schools. Here, religious instructors educated the children of Greek immigrants, teaching many of them to read and write Greek. The first Greek Orthodox church in America was built in 1866 in New Orleans. The second and third churches were built in 1891 and 1898 in New York and Chicago. By the end of World War I in 1918, 130 Greek Orthodox churches were thriving in cities across the United States from Lowell, Massachusetts, to Portland, Oregon. ❁

Opposite: *Many Greek immigrants came to the United States to find work in hopes of being able to return to Greece with the money they earned. These immigrant men helped build the Rensselaer & Pittsfield Electric Railway near Troy, New York, about 1900.*

Chapter Three

Becoming
Greek Americans

A Troubled Path

An Un-American Test

Many of the more than 300,000 Greeks who came to America in the first two decades of the 20th century were reluctant to give up ties to their homeland. The pull of a new way of life in America was not as strong as the urge to return to a relatively young Greek nation with money earned in the United States.

Another reason that many Greeks wanted to return to Greece was the attitude of many Americans about the so-called immigrant invasion. By the mid-1890s, American Protestants, who were generally the wealthiest and best educated Americans, were alarmed at the waves of Roman Catholic, Greek Orthodox, and Jewish immigrants entering the country. A strong prejudice arose against "inferior" people from southern Europe such as Italians and Greeks.

In 1894, a group of young men from Harvard University in Cambridge, Massachusetts, founded the Immigration Restriction League (IRL). The founder of the group stated that all Americans had to decide whether the United States should be populated with "British, German, and Scandinavian stock, historically free . . . or by inferior races . . . down-trodden and . . . stagnant."

The IRL had powerful influence with the public as well as leaders of the U.S. government in the 20 years between its

It's a Fact!

The Immigration Act of 1882 required each new immigrant to pay a "head tax" of 50 cents. That would be equal to about nine dollars today. It also blocked entry into the United States of people who were considered to be idiots, lunatics, convicts, and anyone who was likely to need public assistance to live.

founding and the outbreak of World War I. To keep out "undesir-ables," the IRL proposed a law requiring all immigrants to pass a literacy test. Under this proposal, immigrants over 14 years of age who wanted to come into the United States would have to prove that they could read and write. They did not have to know English if they could read and write their native language.

Although the test seemed reasonable to many educated Americans, it was aimed at immigrants from Italy and Greece. The majority of those people had come from extreme poverty, and most had never gone to school.

The IRL literacy test was approved by Congress several times. Three different presidents, however, vetoed (refused to sign) the act. President Grover Cleveland, who first vetoed the act in 1895, called it "narrow and un-American." Nevertheless, the IRL pressed for the literacy test, while a large segment of the American public adopted anti-immigrant attitudes toward newcomers from southern Europe.

Bloodshed in the Homeland

The pull felt by Greek immigrants between loyalty to their culture and the desire for a better life became more powerful in the first decades of the 20th century. At that time the Ottoman Empire was near collapse, and Turkey was on the edge of civil war. There were still millions of Greeks living in Turkey and throughout the region from the Middle East to the Balkan Peninsula north of Greece.

This period was marked by almost constant warfare between groups seeking control of the areas once under Ottoman control. There were mass killings, called genocide, of certain ethnic groups due to their religion or national origin. Among the millions killed were Armenians and Greeks living in Turkey. The Greeks refer to this period as "the Hellenic Genocide."

An Immigrant's Flight

In the book *Out of the Balkans*, author Jason Mavrovitis describes the escape of his grandmother, Eleni Zissis, from the family's home in the mainly Greek city of Anchialos in the Balkan nation of Bulgaria.

On the night of July 30, 1906, Bulgarian . . . mobs slaughtered four thousand of its six thousand Greek inhabitants of Anchialos. In the terror, Eleni, and her husband, Stefan, were forced to flee. Clinging to their baby, Evangelia, and carrying what few belongings they could, they joined Greek families who ran through the streets toward the docks and small boats that held hope of escape.

Stefan stumbled and fell. The press of humanity trampled him to death and pushed Eleni and her child into the sea. Greek fishermen picked them out of the water and for several days carried them south . . . into the Aegean Sea.

With dread . . . and despair, Eleni retraced the route of her ancient ancestors. She was at sea with the crew of a fishing boat. A destitute widow with an infant and an unknowable future, she had one purpose—to survive.

This bloodshed spread to the Balkan Peninsula, an area known as the "volcano of Europe." It was called this because of the ethnic rivalries and nationalistic hatred that had plagued it for centuries. As the violence continued into 1912, Greece eventually joined several Balkan countries in a war against Turkey. Inspired by patriotic feelings about Greece and their traditional hatred of Ottoman Turkey, more than 45,000 Greek-American immigrants returned to Greece to fight in the Balkan Wars of 1912–1913.

*Greek troops prepare to fight in the Balkan Wars. Members of the Balkan
League (Serbia, Bulgaria, Greece, and Montenegro) fought against the
repressive Ottoman Empire (Turkey). Greece emerged victorious from this
conflict with its territory substantially enlarged.*

Many of these young men were still in the Balkan area
when World War I broke out there in 1914. The deadliest war
in history to that point, World War I was sparked by the
assassination of a German duke in the Balkan city of Sarajevo.
Within a matter of weeks in August 1914, world powers had
formed alliances and declared war. Much of the fighting took
place in the Balkan Peninsula and in Turkey, where Greeks had
lived for centuries.

During the war, Greece allied with Great Britain, France,
Russia, and other nations against the so-called Central Powers.
These included Germany, Austria-Hungary, and Turkey. The

United States entered the fighting in 1917 on the side of Great Britain and France. Thousands of Greek immigrants fought in the U.S. armed forces until the war ended with the defeat of the Central Powers in 1918.

World War I took a tremendous toll not only on armies but on civilians as well. Millions of men, women, and children of Greek descent were killed during the first two decades of the 20th century. Those Greeks who had traditionally lived in Turkey and survived the fighting soon faced another crisis. They were forced to leave Turkey and go to Greece, a "foreign" nation to many Greeks whose roots were in Turkey. Suddenly, Greece faced a refugee crisis for which it was completely unprepared.

Greek refugees board a passenger vessel to escape the destruction and unstable conditions in Greece following World War I.

The sudden flood of refugees from Turkey into Greece became known to Greeks as the "Asia Minor Catastrophe." (Asia Minor is the region of Turkey on the Asian continent.) As a result of the Balkan Wars, Greece was already sheltering many refugees. More than 300,000 had fled to Greece in 1913 alone. Yet that number was small compared to the refugees of the catastrophe that followed Turkey's defeat in World War I. Although the exact number of refugees is uncertain, it is believed that approximately 1.3 million ethnic Greeks fled to their traditional homeland. This enormous mass of people caused the population of Greece to rise by more than 25 percent by 1920.

The Greek government and Greek citizens tried to help the refugees, but there were simply too many. The nation had borrowed enormous amounts of money from European powers in the 1800s, and it still owed that money. Greece had no funds to assist penniless refugees. Diseases spread through the camps where the refugees lived, killing hundreds of thousands. The cost of settling and caring for the refugees, most of whom had fled poverty and hatred with little more than the clothes they wore, was more than the nation could afford. As it had during other times of economic distress, Greece turned to other countries for help.

Even before the flood of refugees, however, Greece was not a stable country. In addition to its long-lasting financial problems, the nation was torn by war and divided by political rivalries. There was not enough public support to take in more than a million new citizens. American diplomat Henry Morganthau observed the crisis and wrote:

> *A nation only five million strong, never blessed with . . . natural resources . . . impoverished by . . . years of . . . warfare . . . native Greeks had suddenly thrust upon them their . . . brethren from Asia Minor, in numbers equal to one fourth of their own population.*

It was only a matter of time before tensions arose between refugees and native Greek citizens. In some ways, those tensions were similar to those that Greek immigrants to the United States had faced from American citizens. Those living at the poorest levels of society in Greek cities felt that the refugees were taking jobs that they needed to survive. Refugees and natives disagreed over land ownership in rural areas. Tension also arose between Greeks and refugees about "Greekness." Some Greeks considered the refugees ignorant because they were comfortable speaking Turkish and not Greek.

With such tensions disrupting Greece in the years after World War I, many Greeks, both returned immigrants and natives, began to feel the pull of the United States. Because of that, the years between 1919 and 1924 saw the greatest Greek immigration to the United States. During that five-year period, more than 300,000 ethnic Greeks immigrated to the United States. More than half of those immigrants came from Turkey.

The new Greek immigrants to the United States differed from the immigrants of earlier years. The first wave of immigrants had been made up mostly of men, with a large percentage of them planning to return to Greece. After World War I, however, the vast majority of Greek immigrants gave up plans of earning American dollars to buy Greek land. Instead, they went to America to establish themselves as Greek Americans. This changing attitude was demonstrated by the fact that many Greek women, as well as entire families, were among the postwar immigrants. With the arrival of women, children, and extended families, a greater sense of Greek culture began to arise in the United States.

It's a Fact!

The peace agreement that ended the Second Balkan War made southern Macedonia and the island of Crete part of Greece.

Greek Organizations

A s the number of Greek immigrants increased, "Greek Towns" became more common across the United States. In addition to socializing through their churches and families, many Greeks could now also spend time at the various clubs and organizations that formed in these communities. Many of the early clubs were simply groups of Greek immigrants who had emigrated from the same island, city, or region of Greece. Greeks who had come from Turkey and other regions outside of Greece also had social clubs to maintain a connection with their own heritage.

Although the first Greek social clubs had been organized as early as 1905, they began to grow rapidly in the 1920s. These organizations were highly valued in the areas where immigrants settled because the social events they sponsored decreased the isolation many felt in their daily lives.

Many Greeks had come to the United States at a time when their homeland was in upheaval. Therefore the focus of many of the organizations turned to politics. Eventually, the Greek immigrant population began to separate into two opposing viewpoints. Some of the more traditional Greeks supported a conservative point of view toward the idea of "Greekness." For these people, it was important to speak Greek as much as possible, to strictly follow the teachings of the Greek Orthodox Church, and to marry only other Greeks. Other, more liberal Greeks, were likely to be in favor of assimilation. In their view, this meant speaking English, accepting other faiths, and allowing marriage with people of other ethnic groups.

Two national Greek immigrant organizations that were founded in the early 1920s represented these opposing points of view. The Greek American Progressive Association (GAPA) was a conservative group that was firmly against assimilating into the larger American society. Most GAPA members were Greeks who had come to the United States directly from their homeland.

In contrast to GAPA was the American Hellenic Educational Progressive Association (AHEPA). The term "Hellenic" was taken from the word used by ancient Greeks for their country–Hellas. AHEPA had a liberal approach to assimilation. Although AHEPA members were proud of the achievements of ancient Greek civilization, the organization did not require members to belong to the Greek Orthodox Church at all. Many of the original founders of AHEPA were Greeks who had come to the United States from areas outside of Greece.

A Greek-American Childhood in the 1920s

Greek-American sculptor Andrew Saffas was born in Kansas City, Missouri, in 1922. He grew up with an extended family that included his parents, younger sisters, uncles, an aunt, and his favorite relative, his grandmother. Saffas recalls his early years.

As a young boy, I had a wonderful relationship with my maternal grandmother, my Yiayia, Marigo, whom I loved very much. She … frequently gave me money for ice cream, but most of all, I was enthralled by her interesting stories. I was often quite mischievous, and not very obedient, teasing my younger sisters. My mother … would chase after me

brandishing her felt slipper (pandofla), and I would run and hide behind my Yiayia and peek at my mother from one side, or the other, dodging the slipper, as Yiayia [said] … "Min piraxis to ped!" ("Don't touch the child!"). As the first born and only son, I was the pride and joy (the Kamari) of the family.

We celebrated Easter with the traditional, spit-roasted lamb. Yiayia, Mom and my Aunt Virginia would prepare … large quantities of red eggs to crack as we proclaimed, "Christos Anesti!" (Christ is risen). After the feast, we would take the translucent, triangular-shaped [lamb] shoulder-bone to Yiayia, who would "read" the future.

Because few Greek women came to America early on, coffeehouses such as this one in Ambridge, Pennsylvania, were like home for many Greek men.

The disagreements between the two largest Greek-American organizations were fierce. By the end of the 1920s, however, there was little doubt that AHEPA was the more popular organization with most Greeks. And as was the case with many other ethnic immigrant groups, knowledge of their native language soon faded. This happened because at home, Greek was spoken only by older family members, and children were encouraged to speak English. Also, in American schools, only English was spoken. While Greek tradition was usually kept alive in homes, churches, and coffeehouses, the Americanization of Greek immigrants was well under way by the 1930s.

During the 1930s, one of the largest Greek immigrant communities in the United States was located in Chicago. In *Out of the Balkans,* Jason Mavrovitis details his mother's life as a new immigrant. After arriving in New York in 1912, Evangelia Mavrovitis settled in Chicago. Mavrovitis describes the environment in which his mother settled:

Chicago . . . then . . . held the largest Greek population in America. [She] . . . lived in Chicago's 19th Ward, a section of tenements on the old West side. Italians, Greeks and Bulgarians had large colonies bordering Halsted Street. The shops lining the area's crowded sidewalks displayed signs in the languages of their immigrant customers. Chicago's first Greek Orthodox Church, Holy Trinity, was at Halsted and Harrison Streets, in the neighborhood still called "Greek Town." A few blocks to the south . . . was the Maxwell Street Market where vendors sold potatoes, pots, pans, shoes, onions and fresh fish. On their day free from work, the immigrants flocked to the market.

Chicago social worker Grace Abbot wrote about daily life in Chicago's Greek Town in 1927.

The largest settlement of Chicago Greeks is in the nineteenth ward. . . . Here is a Greek Orthodox Church; a school in which children are taught little English, some Greek, much of the achievements of Hellas. . . . Here, too, is the combination of Greek bank, ticket office, notary public, and employment agency; and the coffee houses, where the men drink black coffee, play cards . . . and in the evening sing . . . Greek [songs] or—evidence of their Americanization—listen to the phonograph [record player].

For Greek Americans, the 1920s was a decade during which they looked ahead to the future. Few immigrant families planned to return to Greece. Most hoped to find a way to fit into American society. As it happened, however, some anti-immigrant groups had different ideas about who was American and who was not. ❖

Opposite: In this newspaper cartoon, rich men block a new immigrant while their shadows show their own immigrant heritage.

Chapter Four

The Door Is Closed

A Time of War and Poverty

A New Quota

Despite more than 20 years of constant pressure, the Immigration Restriction League failed to pass a law that required immigrants to pass a literacy test. As World War I came to an end, however, the IRL was finally able to force through the immigration restriction it had long sought. Even though President Woodrow Wilson vetoed it, the so-called literacy law was passed in 1919. The law required all adult immigrants to be able to read in their native language. In families, only the husband was required to be literate.

Still, the law did little to keep immigrants out of the United States. When the IRL had first proposed the law in 1895, many European immigrants were illiterate. By 1919, however, most of them could read. Of the 800,000 immigrants who came to the United States (from all nations) between 1920 and 1921, only 1,450 were barred because they failed the test.

Nevertheless, the IRL's relentless anti-immigrant tactics had stirred up strong anti-immigrant feelings in the United States. By the early 1920s, with Europe in ruins after World War I, the IRL spread fears that the United States would soon became an enormous refugee camp for displaced persons.

Responding to these fears, Congress passed a quota plan in 1921. A quota limited the number of immigrants entering the United States from certain regions. Immigrants from southern Europe, which included all Greeks from inside or outside Greece, were limited to 3 percent of the number already in the United States in 1910. In other words, because the U.S. census (population count) listed about 300,000 Greek Americans among the population, no more than 10,000 Greeks, or 3 percent of the Greek-American population, would be allowed to enter in a year.

Eventually, this had the effect of cutting the number of Greek immigrants to the United States from about 25,000 per year to fewer than 5,000.

This quota reduced the total number of immigrants allowed into the United States from Europe to about 600,000 in all. The ethnic groups with the largest percentage allowed into the country under the quota were the British, Germans, and Scandinavians. These groups were allowed to immigrate in greater numbers because they were the ethnic groups with the largest number of members currently living in the United States.

Yet even these quotas did not limit immigration enough for many Americans at the time. The so-called nativist American groups such as the IRL wanted to further reduce the quotas of immigrants allowed. In 1924, Congressman Albert Johnson, chairman of the U.S. House Committee on Immigration, spoke out about his concerns.

Our cherished institutions [are] diluted by alien blood. . . . The United States is our land. . . . The . . . welcome to all peoples, the . . . indiscriminate acceptance of all races, has definitely ended.

Greek Immigration to America

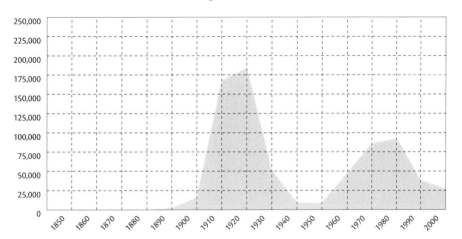

Johnson was the leading author of the Immigration Act of 1924, also known as the National Origins act. This legislation lowered the quota of immigrants allowed into the United States from Europe from 3 percent to 2 percent. And instead of basing that percentage on the most recent census of 1920, Congress based the quota on the 1890 census.

This act served to close the door on immigrants from places other than northern Europe, since in 1890, northern Europeans made up the majority of immigrants in the United States. No European group was more affected by the law than the Greeks, who represented only a small fraction of the immigrant population in 1890.

The Great Depression

T he Immigration Act of 1924 ended an era of more than 40 years of heavy immigration to the United States. The flood of newcomers to America was reduced to a trickle. Under the quota system based on the 1890 census, for example, the number of Italians allowed each year fell from 40,000 to fewer than 4,000. For Greeks, the number of immigrants allowed under the quota fell to fewer than 1,000 people per year.

Although supporters of the quota system fully intended to shut the door to the United States, another event did more to stop the arrival of immigrants. That event was the Great Depression of 1929. This dark period in the American economy began over a five-day period from October 24 to October 29, 1929, when the stock market collapsed. Stocks were parts of companies, also known as shares, which could be bought by the public. If a company made profits, the value of the shares rose. Some stock investors made millions of dollars almost overnight in the 1920s.

*Greek sailors gather on a street hoping to find work during
the Great Depression.*

In general, most of the investors in stocks were wealthy. The lure of making quick money, however, also pulled in people who could not afford to lose. One was Greek immigrant George Mehales. Mehales was a restaurant owner in Spartanburg, South Carolina, who had come to the United States in 1909. His story was typical of many of the poorest investors:

> *One of my customers showed me how much money he was making in the market. . . . It looked good to me, and I bit with what you folks [Americans] call "hook, line and sinker." . . . The first day of October in 1929 made me feel like I was rich. . . . By the end of the month . . . I was wiped out. . . . I considered killing myself, 'cause I had nothing left.*

By early 1930, businesses and banks across the country had failed. By 1932, one of every four American workers was jobless. All Americans suffered during the depression, and immigrants were among those hit hardest. Greeks, with strong family, social, and religious traditions, relied on each other to make it through the difficult years.

Jason Mavrovitis describes life in his community in *Out of the Balkans*. Growing up during the depression in New York City, his father and many other Greeks worked in the garment industry. They lived in tightly packed apartment buildings called tenements:

> *Greeks who toiled in the garment industry clustered together close to their workplaces, seeking community and safety for their families. They lived in small two or three room flats heated by coal fired kitchen ovens, and, if they could afford it, by portable kerosene heaters. On hot, humid New York summer nights they gathered on rooftops, sleeping on mattresses in family groups. Only in the best of circumstances did a flat have its own toilet and a tub where a bath could be taken with water heated in the kitchen. Yet compared to the refugee camps in Greece this was luxury.*

Mavrovitis also recalls the time he spent with his sister helping to earn money.

> *Nitsa and I spent many hours at the kitchen table with Mom while she taught us to mark a pattern on material and to cut, baste, and sew by hand and at the professional Singer Sewing Machine. Making dresses, skirts and blouses was a game for us.*

It's a Fact!

One of the biggest celebrities in Greek-American communities of the 1930s was a professional wrestler named Jim Londos. Nicknamed "The Golden Greek," Londos was the world heavyweight wrestling champion in 1934.

Like many in the Greek community, however, Mavrovitis's mother helped other struggling immigrants.

[She] gave at every opportunity of herself and of her resources. At Christmas she would send me out anonymously with packages of food and gifts for poor Greek families. When I was seven and eight she loaded me with two huge shopping bags every two or three weeks and sent me out to walk a mile or more to the Staten Island Ferry, travel across the bay, take a train, and deliver food to an old couple that were half blind and lived on a small farm [on] the Island.

In Greek families during the depression, if parents worked, they usually made arrangements so that one parent was home to take care of the children. If that was impossible, the crowded conditions of tenement life usually meant that someone was nearby to watch over the youngest children. Often older aunts and an extended family of friends provided child care. Through this network, the traditions of the Greek homeland and culture were passed down to the first U.S.-born Greek Americans. These bonds linked generations of Greeks and bridged the distance between the "old country" and the new.

Outside the home, community organizations and social clubs provided a place for formal and informal gatherings. Although these groups met for conversation and coffee, they also took on the task of helping the less fortunate in the community. Many of these groups were organized by women. The Myrophoros (Greek for "carrying the poor") and the Philoptochos organizations helped families in need during the depression. The Greek-American League of Women Voters, the Muses of Helicon, the Daughters of Penelope, and other organizations all arose in Greek communities of the 1930s. In many ways, they paved the way for the entry of Greek women into politics several decades later.

Most important, of course, the church was a beacon of hope to Greeks during the dark days of the depression. While not all Greek Americans shared the same strong religious beliefs, the church was still the center of community life for everyone. In the Greek Orthodox Church, the most important services were centered on family events such as births, marriages, and deaths. The religious traditions associated with these important events gave Greeks a sense of connection with the customs and traditions of their homeland. Gifts were given to parents after the naming of a child at church. Wedding celebrations at the church usually included music played on a bouzouki, an instrument resembling a banjo, as well as Greek pastries and lines of dancers. Funerals were marked with traditional foods and music as well.

The Terrible Decade

While the Greek-American immigrant community struggled through the depression, political unrest again spread over Greece and much of Europe. In 1936, the Greek general Ioannis Metaxas was appointed as minister of war and then prime minister. Metaxas, who dreamed of creating a "New Greek Empire," immediately canceled parliament's session and took absolute power.

Greek general and dictator Ioannis Metaxas (1871–1941)

Next, Metaxas suspended the human rights guaranteed by the Greek constitution. By doing so, he became the dictator of Greece. Political parties and labor unions were abolished. Political opponents were arrested. Newspapers could no longer print anything that Metaxas did not approve of. Secret police helped Metaxas hold onto power. More than 30,000 Greeks were arrested and thrown out of the country because of their political views. Torture was used to gain confessions from Metaxas's political opponents.

At that time, Metaxas was following a model of government known as fascism, which had taken hold in Germany and Italy. The rule of Adolf Hitler and the Nazis in Germany and Benito Mussolini in Italy threatened all of Europe. Despite Metaxas's dreams of military conquest, both Germany and Italy were much more powerful than Greece. Both nations knew that Greece was strategically important for their own dreams of empire.

The *Nea Hellas*

As the threat of war grew stronger in Europe and political rule in Greece became increasingly severe, many Greeks attempted to leave. Many immigrants traveled by sea from the Greek port of Piraeus on a 14-day journey to New York City. Most of these voyagers traveled on one large ocean liner, the *Nea Hellas* ("New Greece"). The ship departed on its first voyage in May 1939, four months before the outbreak of World War II.

Greek American Nicholas Dinos of Athens, Ohio, was five years old in 1939, when his mother and father took him and his younger sister, Bette, to Greece for a family visit. The family was in Greece when the war began and made their return passage on the *Nea Hellas*.

We were [followed] by a German submarine, which caused us all to be forced to stay on deck with life preservers on for a couple of days and nights. I still remember the 17-day trip. My mother kept telling me to remember lifeboat No. 9, which was the boat she was assigned to. I later found out she intended to get Bette and me on it, and then stay with my father, even if it meant that we would be orphaned.

In October 1940, Italy demanded that Greece allow Italian forces to occupy locations on Greek soil. Metaxas refused, and Greece was once again plunged into war when Italian forces invaded the country. Metaxas died shortly after the invasion by Italy, which in turn was followed by a German attack in 1941.

Athens fell to the German invaders. By June 1941, Greece had been divided between Germany and Italy. The Germans controlled important cultural and strategic positions from the capital, Athens, to the border with Turkey, as well as the Aegean Islands. Italian forces occupied the rest of Greece.

As they did in other areas they conquered, German forces took control of Greece's resources for their own war effort. By the winter of 1941–1942, food shortages had led to a famine that killed as many as 100,000 Greeks. Resistance movements arose and Greeks with differing political views joined together to become allies to fight the Germans. The resistance was so effective that by 1943, the Germans declared that 50 Greeks would be executed for every German soldier that was killed. Until the war ended in 1945, Greece was brutalized by the Germans. Whole villages were destroyed. Almost the entire population of Jewish people in Greece, more than 50,000, was sent to the Auschwitz death camp in Poland.

Conditions in Greece became even worse after the end in the war in 1945. The political opponents who had fought together against the Germans turned on each other and fought for control of the nation. In late 1946, a force called the Democratic Army of Greece (DAG) began attacks against the

It's a Fact!

Although most Jewish people either fled Greece or were sent to concentration camps during the German occupation, a few remained behind. They were hidden by Christians and joined resistance forces that hid in the mountains and attacked the Germans.

national army. The DAG, however, was not "democratic" in the traditional sense. Instead, it was led by leaders of the Communist Party, which favored a political system that did not allow the ownership of private property. The conflicts between the DAG and the national forces, the actual representatives of a democratic government, led to the bloody Greek Civil War, which began in the winter of 1946–1947.

The Cold War

At the end of World War II, the Soviet Union, which had been allied with the United States against the Nazis, controlled most of eastern Europe. This included most of the Balkan Peninsula bordering Greece. In 1946, Soviet leader Joseph Stalin gave a speech in which he declared that democratic nations could never live side by side with nations such as his that were ruled by communism. Around the same time, an American diplomat in Moscow wrote a memo in which he called communism a danger to the free world. It was now clear that the communism of the Soviet Union and the democracy of the United States and elsewhere, two vastly different systems of government, were in conflict.

This conflict became known as the cold war. The term *cold war* referred to a conflict between large, powerful nations that involved political tension but not all-out war. Smaller countries such as Greece became political battlegrounds for the opposing powers as they fought to influence the governments of the smaller countries. During World War II, Greeks of all political views had fought side by side against the Nazis. After World War II, however, Greece became the first cold war battleground. Suddenly, Greeks were fighting other Greeks with opposing political views. Greece was an obvious choice for a cold war battle-ground because Communist-controlled nations to the north such as Yugoslavia (now the republics of Bosnia, Croatia, and Serbia, among others) and Bulgaria could easily send military support to Greek Communist forces.

The Greek Civil War was marked by brutality on both sides. Innocent civilians were tortured and murdered. Because the DAG was a Communist army, the war was also an international concern. At that time, Europe and the United States feared that any Communist conflict would be supported by Joseph Stalin, the leader of the Soviet Union. Greece was the first European country to become a battleground in this struggle.

In 1947, responding to the crisis in Greece, U.S. president Harry S. Truman proclaimed the Truman Doctrine, a policy that tried to stop communism from spreading to other countries. To fulfil the commitment to help Greece become a democracy, the United States offered the country $400 million in aid. The assistance from the United States helped defeat the Communist forces and the civil war ended in 1949.

Greece, however, was a nation in ruins after a terrible decade. In addition to the more than 500,000 killed in World War II, more than 80,000 Greeks died in the civil war and almost 1 million more became refugees. Soon after the Truman Doctrine was announced, Congress passed the Displaced Persons Act in 1948. The law allowed certain Greeks to immigrate despite the quota restrictions. For example, many of these new immigrants were orphans whose parents had been killed in the conflicts in Greece. Others were refugees from the fighting who had relatives in the United States. For a period from the late 1940s into the 1950s, more than 50,000 Greeks came to the United States without being counted against the quota set in 1924. Although these refugees were welcomed into Greek-American communities, they did not open the door for another wave of immigration. The door would remain closed for another decade.

Opposite: *Greek Orthodox priests in Astoria, Queens, New York*

Chapter Five

The Door
Opens Again

Finding a Place in America

Greek American Council

For Greek Americans, the bloody civil war in their homeland caused both heartache and anger. Many Greeks living in the United States had relatives trapped in the fighting. At the same time, political differences about the war were reflected in Greek-American political organizations. The Greek American Council (GAC) was formed to win support for a return to parliamentary democracy in Greece. Under that system, the people would be able to elect leaders for the legislative branch of the government. The GAC opposed both the Communists as well as the politicians remaining from the Metaxas era. Another Greek-American group, known as the EAM (Ethnikon Apeleutheritikon Metopon), was organized to support the formation of a new democratic government in Greece similar to that of the United States.

Although these groups were formed specifically to give Greek Americans a voice in the affairs of their homeland, the two largest Greek American organizations took no position on the civil war. AHEPA and GAPA focused on putting pressure on the U.S. Congress to change immigration laws that had remained basically unchanged since 1924.

The Assimilation of the 1950s

In the aftermath of World War II and the civil war in Greece, few Greek Americans considered returning to Greece to live. Instead, they stayed in the United States and continued to establish families and communities. By the 1950s, the number of American-born Greeks, called the "second generation," outnumbered Greek Americans who had been born in Greece (known as the "first generation"). Many in this second generation felt as closely attached to the United States as they did to their ethnic homeland. Although they still faced some prejudice, this prejudice was nowhere near as hostile as that faced by the first generation. Unlike their parents, the second generation had been educated in the United States. That had helped open the door to American society.

U.S. military veterans of Greek descent took advantage of the benefits available to all veterans. They attended colleges and technical schools to further their education. They received government loans to buy homes in areas outside of cities. For the first time, Greek Orthodox churches began to appear in suburbs.

Pushed to succeed, second-generation Greek Americans soon entered occupations such as law, medicine, journalism, and politics. Among second-generation immigrant groups, during the 1950s the incomes of second-generation Greek Americans were exceeded only by those of second-generation Lithuanians, Japanese, and Russians. Greek-American employment rates were the highest of all second-generation groups. The percentage of that group performing manual labor was among the lowest for any group.

The 1950s was a decade of achievement as well as assimilation for Greek Americans. Among the great achievements in medicine of the 1950s was the development of the "Pap" test for cervical cancer by Dr. George Papanicolaou. Greek Americans also rose to prominence in other fields. Movie director Elia Kazan, born in Istanbul, directed the Academy

Elia Kazan, film and stage director

Award-winning film *On the Waterfront* in 1954. Kazan became one Hollywood's legendary film directors.

The 1950s also marked the first entry of Greek Americans into politics. Several cities across the United States, including San Francisco; St. Paul, Minnesota; Hartford, Connecticut; Syracuse, New York; and Savannah, Georgia, all elected Greek Americans as mayors. The fact that none of these cities had large Greek immigrant populations was evidence that Greek Americans were rapidly becoming assimilated.

Dove Bars

In the 1950s, Chicago had one of the largest Greek-American communities in the United States. Among the small Greek-owned businesses there was a candy store owned by Leo Stefanos. Stefanos often worried when his two young sons chased the neighborhood ice cream truck down the street to buy sweet treats. He also felt slightly jealous that his boys wanted another vendor's product. He spent months developing his own ice cream treat, which became the chocolate-covered DoveBar in 1956. Stefanos's invention made him a millionaire when the right to manufacture the DoveBar was bought by an international candy company in 1963.

A Campaign for Change

D espite the great success achieved by Greek Americans, immigration laws continued to limit the number of immigrants from Greece and other nations into the United States. That limit, based on a strict 1924 law, was tightened further in 1952 with the passage of the McCarren-Walter Act. This legislation arose during the so-called Communist scare of the early 1950s. At that time many Americans feared that Communists were working in the U.S. government. In addition, many Americans and lawmakers feared that some immigrants might be Communist spies.

Despite President Truman's veto, the McCarren-Walter Act was passed by Congress due to concerns about "internal security." The law kept the same quota restrictions as the 1924 immigration act. In addition, however, it demanded that all immigrants pass a complicated loyalty test. It also gave the U.S. attorney general the power to deport (send out of the country) any immigrants who were accused of associating with Communist groups, even after the immigrants had become American citizens.

The passage of the McCarren-Walter act angered many immigrant organizations. Among these, AHEPA took the lead in trying to get the law repealed. Most immigrants from Greece were still entering as non-quota "displaced persons." Under the strict law, the quota for others remained just 308 immigrants from Greece per year. AHEPA continued to work against the act throughout the 1950s. Even with the quota restrictions in place, however, more than 4,000 Greeks came to the United States each year between 1948 and 1960.

In the early 1960s, the government of Greece was again disrupted by a military takeover as it had been during the Metaxas era before World War II. By 1963, army and police units began to intimidate voters who wanted a democratic government. Politicians were assassinated by security forces. By the mid-1960s, conservative career military officers had named themselves the "protectors" of Greece. Supporters of the officers were generally uneducated military men who terrorized people to get their way.

This military government claimed that Greece was "morally sick." It passed a series of strict laws that banned women from wearing short skirts and required all men to have short military haircuts. Secret police prowled through every level of society, and torture was widespread. Greece became an international outcast because it had become a nation that denied its own citizens basic rights.

The brutal scene in Greece made it even more critical for AHEPA to pressure Congress to remove the immigration quotas. Thousands of Greeks, many of them educators, writers, and artists, were desperate to flee the rule of what became known as "the Colonels."

An armored vehicle patrols a street in Athens, Greece, in 1967 during the takeover of the country by military leaders.

Finally, in 1965, the efforts of AHEPA and other immigrant organizations paid off. Congress passed the Immigration Act of 1965, which was signed into law by President Lyndon Johnson. Under the act, 120,000 immigrants were allowed into the United States each year from nations in the Western Hemisphere. Another 170,000 were allowed from all other nations, but not more than 20,000 of these immigrants could come from any single country. Families of people already in the United States, educated workers, and refugees (people left homeless by war or political unrest) were given high priority.

In effect, the 1965 legislation ended the quota system. The family connection allowance was a great benefit to Greek immigrants because many of those who hoped to immigrate had relatives already living in the United States. Not only did this speed their entry, it also aided them in the process of assimilation.

Pushed out of Greece by economic instability and political repression, more than 140,000 Greeks came to the United States between 1965 and 1975 alone. This was the largest wave of immigrants from Greece in any 10-year period since before World War I. The political situation in Greece at the time resulted in a different class of immigrant coming to the United States. In this group, there was a much higher percentage of educated professionals and skilled workers. Because of their connections with Greek Americans already in the United States, the new arrivals found jobs in food-service industries, skilled trades such as engineering, and sales and service work, such as health care. New immigrants with fewer skills found work in domestic service, agriculture, and, largely in New York City, as taxi cab drivers.

Although this new wave of Greek immigrants faced less prejudice than had their fellow Greeks in the early 20th century, they still faced a period of adjustment in the United States. More than 90 percent of the people who came to the United

States did not speak English. Most settled in Queens, New York, which had the largest population of Greek immigrants in New York City. As a result, a number of private immigrant assistance organizations were formed in the greater New York region. The most well known was the Hellenic American Neighborhood Action Committee (HANAC). HANAC collected funds to create immigrant-orientation programs that taught English as a second language. HANAC also created job-placement programs as well as an economic assistance program for small businesses.

The organizational skills of Greek Americans in the 1960s were based on their traditional beliefs that the community should help all of its members. The 1960s also marked the entry of Greek Americans into national politics, an area in which they could put those beliefs into action to benefit people outside the community. Greeks always had a great deal of enthusiasm for politics, from their ancient empire to AHEPA. Although Greek immigrants who ran for office in local elections were often successful due to "Greek Town" community support, success on the national scene eluded Greek Americans until the 1960s.

At the beginning of that decade, John Brademas of Indiana and Paul Sarbanes of Maryland became the first Greek Americans elected to the U.S. House of Representatives. Sarbanes served several terms as a representative and was elected U.S. senator in 1977. In 1967, Spiro T. Agnew was elected governor of Maryland. The following year, he became the vice president of the United States under President Richard Nixon.

Few American politicians of the 1960s and early 1970s were more controversial than Spiro T. Agnew. Born in the Greek community of Baltimore, Maryland, his full last name was Agnostopoulos. Like many second-generation Greek immigrants, he Americanized his name as a young man. An army veteran of World War II, Agnew went to college on the G.I. Bill, which paid the college tuition of service members.

As a lawyer in the 1950s, Agnew was active in Republican politics in Baltimore. In 1962, he was elected the chief executive of Baltimore county. In 1967, Agnew was elected governor of Maryland. In 1969, he became Richard Nixon's vice president.

As Nixon's vice president, Agnew spoke out harshly against those who protested American involvement in the Vietnam War. His speeches became famous when he used phrases such as "effete [weak] intellectual snobs" and "nattering nabobs of negativism" to criticize war protesters. Agnew's conservative political views focused on other countries as well. At a time when the Greek government was run by the hated military group known as the "Colonels," Agnew was the only international politician who visited Greece.

Reelected with Nixon in 1972, Agnew soon received another type of fame. He was charged with having taken bribes when he was Baltimore county executive and governor of Maryland. Agnew became the first vice president to resign from office, in 1973. He was eventually convicted of income tax evasion, or not paying his taxes.

For most Americans, acceptance of Greek Americans did not occur in politics, but in popular culture. By the early 1960s, several Greek-American professional athletes had gained national fame. Greek American Johnny Unitas led pro football's Baltimore Colts to two championships. He set a number of professional records and was widely considered one of the best quarterbacks ever to play the game.

Spiro T. Agnew was often outspoken. He loved bashing the media before he resigned as vice president in 1973.

Baltimore Colts quarterback John Unitas stands over the center during a game in Memorial Stadium, Baltimore, Maryland.

Another Greek American, Alex Karras, played defensive tackle for the Detroit Lions. In a 1964 movie about pro football called *Paper Lion,* Karras became a star for his sense of humor as well as his football skills. He went on to act in more movies and was a sports broadcaster.

Greek-American athletes also became fan favorites in baseball. In the late 1950s and early 1960s, two Greek Americans were key players for the Baltimore Orioles, one of baseball's best teams. Pitcher Milt Pappas pitched nine seasons for the Orioles and never had a losing season. In 1963, Pappas pitched a no-hit game. The catcher for that game, and for many other Orioles games, was Greek American Gus Triandos, one of baseball's all-time great catchers.

Speaking Greek

Perhaps the most interesting aspect of Greek is its influence over thousands of years on the English language. Many of the prefixes (beginnings of words), suffixes (ends of words), and roots of English words originally came from ancient Greek. Below are some examples of the "assimilation" of Greek into English.

GREEK PREFIXES

bio: means "life, living organism"; examples—biology, biography

hyper: means "excessive"; examples—hyperactive, hypersensitive

micro: means "small"; examples—microscope, microbe

ped: means "foot"; examples—pedestrian, pedal

therm, thermo: means "heat"; examples—thermometer, thermos

GREEK SUFFIXES

–graph: means "writing"; examples—autograph, seismograph

–meter, –metry: means "measure, measuring"; examples—kilometer, geometry

–phobic, –phobia: means "fear"; examples—claustrophobic, arachnophobia

GREEK ROOTS

chron: means "time"; examples—chronology, synchronize

dem: means "people"; examples—democracy, epidemic

path: means "feeling"; examples—sympathy, apathetic

The assimilation of Greek Americans into mainstream American life continued throughout the 1960s. In many ways, this movement was as much a product of the times as it was of the Greek-American people themselves. The 1960s were a time during which many segments of American society began to assert their rights as equal citizens. African Americans, for example, demanded civil rights protection. American women demanded equality in pay, laws, and other areas of American society.

Greek immigrants to the United States during the 1960s left behind a nation that many believed had turned its back on the democratic tradition. Many saw opportunities available to them in the United States that simply did not exist in Greece. Peter Doulis, for example, immigrated to New York in 1966. Like many immigrants of that time, he had relatives living in New York who offered help to get settled. He came with his family and the confidence that his two young children had a brighter future in America. "I knew if I came here I could finish my studies and find a good job afterwards," Doulis said. At the time he left his homeland, he said, "Getting accepted into college in Greece [was] very difficult, and . . . to find a . . . job . . . [in the field] . . . you studied [was] almost impossible."

In some ways, Doulis's hopes for greater opportunity in the United States were like those of the first immigrants in the early 20th century. Unlike those first Greek American immigrants, however, he was not drawn to the United States by exaggerated stories. By the last half of the 20th century, opportunities for Greek Americans were real. ⚎

Opposite: *People wear traditional Greek outfits during a Greek Independence Day celebration.*

Chapter Six

Greek Americans Today

Greek Pride and Achievement

A Wave of New Americans

I n the early 1970s, Greeks continued to immigrate in relatively large numbers to the United States. Almost 60,000
arrived between 1971 and 1975. Almost all of these immigrants
settled in Astoria, Queens, a part of New York City. So many
Greeks came to Astoria that it became known as "Little Athens"
and was the largest Greek community outside of Greece. The
church of Saint Demetrios, in fact, was also home to an elemen-
tary, middle, and high school that was the largest Greek-
American school in the United States.

*Most Greek immigrants have settled
in these states.*

A number of organizations in Astoria, such as the Hellenic American Neighborhood Action Committee (HANAC), arose at this time to help immigrants adjust to life in the United States. Settling in Astoria, however, made it almost unnecessary for new immigrants to assimilate. Spiro Stamatakis, who came to Astoria in 1971, described his first years in the United States. "When I came to Astoria, I never wanted to learn English, but because I wanted to work outside of Astoria, I had to learn English."

Stamatakis took advantage of HANAC classes to learn English, and, in the late 1970s, he sent for his parents, who were still in Greece. They did not speak English, but they felt at home in the community. The streets of Astoria resembled a Greek town, Stamatakis explains. Small children playing in the streets spoke Greek. Butcher shops had skinned goats, a favorite meat in Greece, hanging in their windows. Greek music boomed from Greek nightclubs and diners.

Many of the Greeks who came to Astoria in the 1960s and 1970s planted gardens to remind them of their homeland. "All Greeks, if they have their own homes, they have a garden. And all Greeks plant fig trees. The tree reminds them of their country," Stamatakis says. "Greeks in Astoria like to keep their Greek heritage and their Greek customs."

Greek Americans Assimilate

At the same time that large numbers of new arrivals were coming to the United States from Greece, second-generation Greek Americans were moving into American society at large. As in the previous decades, politics became one important area in which Greek Americans made their presence felt.

Michael Dukakis, who served in the Massachusetts House of Representatives from 1963 to 1970, became the state's governor in 1975. Greek American Paul Tsongas of Lowell, Massachusetts, was elected to the U.S House of Representatives in 1975 and became a U.S. senator from Massachusetts in 1979.

Michael Dukakis and his wife, Kitty, acknowledge the cheers of supporters during his presidential campaign in 1988.

Greek-American women also entered politics during the 1970s. In Maine, Olympia Snowe was elected to the state House of Representatives in 1973. In 1978, Snowe was elected to the U.S. House of Representatives, becoming the youngest Republican woman and the first Greek-American woman ever elected to Congress.

Greek Americans also became more visible in American culture in other ways. In 1961, Greek American George Chakiris won the Academy Award for Best Supporting Actor in the film *West Side Story.* In 1964, Greek American Lila Kedrova won the Academy Award for Best Supporting Actress for her role in the movie *Zorba the Greek.*

One of the most respected actors and film directors of the 1960s and 1970s was Greek American John Cassavetes. He starred in two of the most popular films of the late 1960s, *The Dirty Dozen* and *Rosemary's Baby.* Cassavetes then went on to direct a number of films in which actors were required to make up their own lines as the cameras filmed the scenes. This style of acting, called improvisation, represented a major development in movie making. Cassavetes was nominated for three Academy Awards for acting and directing.

Television also helped to make Greek Americans visible to the public. One of the most popular television and movie stars of the 1970s was first-generation Greek American Telly Savalas. For five years in the mid-1970s, Savalas starred as Kojak, a New York City detective, in a popular police drama. Savalas's brother, Demetrios, also starred in the show.

Immigration Slows

Major changes in the government of Greece in the 1970s brought an end to the second wave of Greek immigration. Many of those immigrants had left Greece to escape the brutal military leadership of the time. In October 1973, however, college students in Greece rebelled against the limits that had been placed on free speech, as well as the ban on public meetings. The students were joined by other Greeks who were angered by serious economic problems that the dictatorship was unable to solve.

The military dictators reacted to these events by calling in the army to stop a student protest march in Athens. Tanks rumbled through the crowds, crushing students and killing dozens. Yet the brutality only weakened the dictators, as millions of Greeks in Greece and around the world demanded an end to the dictatorship.

In November 1974, more than 70 percent of Greek citizens voted to end the monarchy, which had supported the harsh military rule. Even the military forces had grown angry about the brutal methods of their leaders, and they refused to threaten voters. With no king and no military support, the dictatorship was over. For the first time in modern Greek history, its government was a democracy.

The change to a democratic form of government had a large effect on the number of Greeks immigrating to the United States. New political freedom after years of oppression persuaded many Greeks to remain in their homeland rather than leaving for a distant country. Between 1970 and 1980, an average of 11,000 Greek immigrants came to the United States each year. From the early 1980s until the end of the 20th century, the average number of Greek immigrants to the United States fell to about 1,500 per year. Many of these immigrants were family members of immigrants who had come in the second wave, from 1961 to 1980.

Greek-American Successes

By the last decades of the 20th century, Greek Americans had assumed important roles in almost every aspect of American life. In 1988, Michael Dukakis became the first Greek American to run for president, losing to George H. W. Bush.

In 1992, Paul Tsongas ran unsuccessfully for the Democratic nomination for president. During the 1992 presidential election, Greek American George Stephanopoulos served as deputy campaign manager and director of communications for winner Bill Clinton. Stephanopoulos later went on to become a television news reporter and talk show host.

As Greek Americans became more widely assimilated into American society, many second- and third-generation Greek Americans married non-Greeks. Nevertheless, Greek Americans in "mixed" marriages retained their pride in their Greek roots. Olympia Snowe, who married a non-Greek, was selected to complete her husband's term in the Maine House of Representatives after his death. Snowe (her married name) was proud of her Greek heritage. She went on to win several more terms in state government.

Like many Greek Americans, Snowe has made an important contribution to American politics at a national level as well. After serving seven terms in the House of Representatives, she was elected to the U.S. Senate, becoming the first woman, and the first Greek American, in U.S. history to serve in both houses of a state legislature and both houses of Congress.

Greek-American women have also become famous in entertainment. Actress Jennifer Aniston, well-known for her role in the television show *Friends,* spent a year of her childhood living in Greece, the homeland of her mother's family. Greek-American actress Rita Wilson, wife of actor Tom Hanks, was the producer of the 2001 movie *My Big Fat Greek Wedding.*

Nia Verdalos, star of the movie My Big Fat Greek Wedding

Greek Americans also continued to rise to prominence in sports. Pete Sampras was one of the great tennis champions of the 1990s. Eric Karros, first baseman of the Los Angeles Dodgers, was the Rookie of the Year in 1990. In football, 340-pound tackle Tony Siragusa helped the Baltimore Ravens win the Super Bowl in 2000. Bob Costas became one of the most well-known sportscasters in the world.

Successful Greek Americans also became the owners of professional sports teams. Ted Leonsis, founder of America Online (AOL), owned the Washington Wizards professional basketball team. Peter Karmanos, president of the computer company Compuware, bought the Carolina Hurricanes hockey team.

Many of these Greek Americans were first-generation Greeks who had worked their way out of poverty. Alex Spano, billionaire owner of the San Diego Chargers football team, for example, began working at age eight, making pastries at his father's restaurant. The parents of Peter Angelos, the owner of baseball's Baltimore Orioles, arrived in the United States with less than five dollars in their pockets.

Renewing Roots

Greek Americans have been among the most successful immigrant groups to come to the United States during the period from 1880 to 1920. As successful as many have been, most Greek Americans, like most other Americans, live the average lives of ordinary people. Among the first generation of Greek-American immigrants, the desire to be simply "American" was a powerful force. Jason Mavrovitis, who grew up in the 1930s, writes: "In my youth I rebelled against the label 'Greek-American' and disliked attending the Greek speaking, Greek Orthodox Church. I, like my friends in school, considered myself an American."

Later generations of Greek Americans, however, have balanced their American side with their Greek heritage. This return to cultural pride was aided in part by the large second wave of Greeks that came to the United States in the 1960s and 1970s. Giannoula Tsoflias and her husband brought their two young daughters to New York during that time. They settled in Astoria, New York, the largest Greek community in America. For the Tsoflias family, immigration was critical because of political and economic turmoil in Greece at the time. Yet Tsoflias and her husband did not want their daughters to forget their homeland. In Astoria, they had the best of both worlds. "You can hear Greek being spoken everywhere. People yell from one front porch to the other, they come out of the Acropolis coffee house and shout across the street, and cars go by playing Greek music," says Tsoflias.

Other Greek-American communities offer the same opportunity to remain in touch with traditions from Greece. The Boston suburb of Roslindale is home to the largest Greek population in New England. Second-generation Greek American Eleni Vidalis, who has lived in Roslindale all her life, explains the close ties within the community "The Greek community is very proud of its culture," Vidalis says, "very close-knit. They [shop in] Greek-owned places and stores and support each other. You don't need to go outside Roslindale. There's a shoemaker, a dry cleaner, a bakery, and a bookstore."

Vidalis understands why immigrants in the second wave from Greece also sought out places that felt like home. "Your own kind of people are already there. You move to where they speak the language," she explains.

In the center of Roslindale is Alexander the Great Park, with a statue of the famous ancient Greek ruler in the middle of an open field. The sculpture was a gift from the people of Athens and was dedicated during a visit by the mayor of Greece's capital city.

Two chefs cook lambs over charcoal grills at Estiatorio Milos, a Greek restaurant in Queens, New York. Lamb is served after midnight during a traditional meal celebrating the Greek Orthodox Easter.

As in most Greek-American communities, the Greek Orthodox Church in Roslindale is at the center of most activities, whether community members are regular churchgoers or not. St. Nectarios Greek Orthodox Church sits directly across the street from Alexander the Great Park. The church holds classes in Greek language every afternoon. Community festivals, from weddings to christenings to funerals, all take place in the church hall. Whatever the occasion, traditional Greek music, dancing, and food draw many eager participants.

Vidalis describes Greek music as something "you feel in your heart, even if you don't understand the words." There are love songs, ballads about life in Greece, and fast-paced songs that tell of important events in Greek history. All are played on traditional instruments such as the bouzouki, a banjo-like instrument invented during the early Ottoman Empire. Musicians also play the *lavouto*, a metal-stringed Greek guitar, the *baglama*, a small stringed instrument, and the accordion.

Ceremonies and Traditions

Birth, marriage, and death are three phases of life that are the basis for the main religious services of the Greek Orthodox Church. Ceremonies observing these events are celebrated by unique Greek customs and social traditions.

Gifts given to a newborn baby often include silver or gold coins. This tradition is known as *asimo to pethi*, or "silver the child." Other gifts are sometimes given to ward off bad luck, such as a *mati"* which is a small blue stone with a black eye in the center.

When a babies are a few months old, they are baptized in the Greek Orthodox Church. At the ceremony, the baby is baptized by the priest with the assistance of the child's godparent. Godparents are traditionally the *koumbaros* who stood as witnesses for the child's parents' wedding.

A Greek Orthodox wedding service is the same in churches around the world. The hour-long ceremony has several steps, including lighting of candles, crowning of the bride and groom with *stephana*, or crowns linked by a ribbon, and dancing, in which the priest leads the couple around a small table at the front of the church.

Greek-American wedding celebrations include bouzouki music, dancing, and Greek wedding sweets such as baklava, a honey-almond pastry, and *kourabiethes*, or Greek butter cookies.

Following the death of a close family member, Greek women are expected to wear black for up to a year to show respect for the deceased. Men, however, wear only a black armband for up to 40 days following the death of a loved one.

When a family member dies, Greek-American women prepare traditional foods such as *kollyva* (boiled wheat) and *paximadia* (walnut cookies), as well as a traditional lamb dinner.

At almost every event, there is also dancing. Dances include the *tsifteli,* which is like Middle Eastern belly dancing. People also participate in a circle dance called *kalamatiano* and rhythmic, whirling dances known as *hasaposerviko.*

Food is also important at any gathering in the Greek community. Foods might include dolmats, grape leaves rolled and stuffed with rice. Other popular dishes include spanakopita (spinach pie made with buttery phyllo dough and sharp feta cheese) and souvlaki (meat roasted a stick, then sliced and served like a hamburger on thin, crusty pita bread with tomatoes). Casserole-type dishes such as *pastichio,* the Greek version of Italian lasagne, are always popular. So is moussaka, a dish made from eggplant and ground meat.

National Pride

In Greek-American communities, there are many holidays to celebrate. No holiday, however, is more widely celebrated than March 25. It is called Greek Independence Day, and it celebrates the beginning of the revolt against Turkey in 1821. Many cities observe the day with a parade. In many communities, men march wearing the traditional military jackets, kilt-like skirts, and leggings worn by the original freedom fighters.

In addition to parades, there are also traditional dances on Independence Day. Young people learn the dances from older Greek Americans and practice the steps for months. Groups perform on Independence Day both to show their skill and simply for the love of dancing, which is an ageless Greek tradition. In fact, regions of Greece are known by their specific style of music, dance, and dress.

Many Greek Americans, especially children, wear traditional dress with a bandanna and velvet jacket on Greek Independence

Day. Years ago, young people of the first generation of Greek Americans rebelled against wearing traditional clothing on holidays. Today, the second- and third-generation Greek Americans have changed. "My age group didn't want to bother," says Vidalis. "But . . . today's young people are different. They don't Americanize their names. It's Eleni, not Helen, and Dimitri, not Jimmy. You can tell right away if someone's Greek."

Looking Back and Forward

The 2000 census determined that the population of Greek Americans in the United States was 1,153,307. That number represents about 0.4 percent of the American population. Although a large number of those who list themselves as Greek Americans came to the United States in the 1960s and 1970s, most are descended from immigrants who came in the early 20th century.

Whether the ties to Greece are recent or distant, however, the pride in being Greek is deeply felt. In fact, for many Greek Americans, those feelings grew deeper as the 21st century began. Now, many Greek Americans look back with admiration at the determination and courage of the first Greek Americans. At the same time, they look forward to passing on the traditions to the next generation of Greek Americans.

Time Line of Greek Immigration

300 B.C.	Height of the ancient Greek Empire.
ca. A.D. 100–400	Early Christianity is established in Greece.
1453	Constantinople falls to Sultan Mehmed II, leader of the Ottoman Turks.
1768–1776	New Smyrna colony of Greeks in Florida is established and abandoned.
1821–1832	Greece gains independence from the Ottoman Empire.
1866	The first Greek Orthodox Church is built in the United States in New Orleans, Louisiana.
1890–1910	The first large wave of Greek immigrants comes to the United States.
1894	The Immigration Restriction League (IRL) is founded.
1912–1913	The Balkan Wars break out on the peninsula north of Greece.
1914–1918	World War I devastates Europe. Thousands of Greek refugees flee from Turkey.
1919–1924	Period of the greatest Greek immigration to the United States. More than 300,000 ethnic Greeks enter the United States.
1921	Congress passes the first immigration quota to limit the number of immigrants entering the United States from certain regions, including Greece.
1924	Immigration Act of 1924 reduces the percentage of immigrants allowed into the United States from Europe. Greek immigration is reduced to fewer than 1,000 immigrants per year.
1930s	The Great Depression causes economic hardship in the United States.
1940–1941	Italian forces invade Greece. Athens falls to German invaders.
1941	Japanese forces attack Pearl Harbor, Hawaii. The United States enters World War II against Japan, Germany, and Italy.

1945	World War II ends. German forces are driven from Greece.
1946	The Greek Civil War breaks out between the Communist-supported Democratic Army of Greece (DAG) and the Greek army.
1948	Congress passes Displaced Persons Act, which allows some Greeks to immigrate despite the quota restrictions.
1949	The Greek Civil War ends with the defeat of the Communist forces. More than 1 million Greeks become refugees.
1952	The McCarren-Walter Act enforces a loyalty code for all immigrants.
1962	John Brademas of Indiana and Paul Sarbanes of Maryland are the first Greek Americans elected to the U.S. House of Representatives.
1963	Military dictatorship takes control in Greece. Political dissent is crushed.
1965	President Lyndon Johnson signs the Immigration and Nationality Act of 1965.
1965–1975	More than 140,000 Greeks emigrate to the United States.
1968	Spiro T. Agnew becomes the first Greek American elected to the vice presidency of the United States.
1978	Olympia Snowe of Maine is elected to the U.S. House of Representatives and becomes the first Greek-American woman elected to Congress.
1988	Michael Dukakis, former governor of Massachusetts, becomes the first Greek American to run for president.
1992	Greek American George Stephanopoulos serves as deputy campaign manager and director of communications for President Bill Clinton.
2000	U.S. Census lists 1,153,307 Greek Americans in the United States, about 0.4 percent of the American population.
2003	*Middlesex*, a novel by Greek-American author Jeffrey Eugenides, is awarded the Pulitzer Prize for fiction.

Glossary

assimilate To absorb or blend into the way of life of a society.

baklava Greek honey-almond pastry with paper-thin dough.

bouzouki Banjo-like instrument with three strings used in
Greek folk music.

constitution Document outlining the basic principles and laws of a nation.

culture The language, arts, traditions, and beliefs of a society.

emigrate To leave one's homeland to live in another country.

ethnic Having certain racial, national, tribal, religious, or cultural origins.

famine Shortage of food; extended period of widespread hunger.

Hellas Name used by ancient Greeks for their country.

immigrate To come to a foreign country to live.

monarchy Nation ruled by a king or queen.

padrone Person who paid for immigrants to come to America and found
them jobs in return for part of the immigrants' pay.

prejudice Negative opinion formed without just cause.

quota A certain percentage of a total number; a share.

refugee Someone who flees a place for safety reasons, especially to
another country.

souvlaki Greek sandwich of meat roasted on a stick, then sliced and
served on thin bread with tomatoes.

spanakopita Greek spinach pie made with wafer-thin dough
and feta cheese.

steerage Least expensive traveling class on a steamship.

Further Reading

BOOKS

Bryan, Nichol. *Greek Americans*. Edina, Minn.: Checkerboard Library, 2004.

Greene, Meg. *The Greek Americans*. San Diego, Calif.: Lucent Books, 2004.

Monos, Demitros. *The Greek Americans*. Broomall, Pa.:
Chelsea House, 2002.

Papanikolas, Helen. *Small Bird, Tell Me: Stories of Greek Immigrants*. Athens,
Ohio: Ohio University Press, 1994.

Wallner, Rosemary. *Greek Immigrants 1890–1920*. Mankato, Minn.:
Bridgestone Books, 2002.

WEB SITES

Acropolis of America. "The Greek Community of Lowell, Massachusetts."
URL: http://floweringcity.org/intro.htm. Updated on May 26, 2004.

The American Hellenic Education Progressive Association (AHEPA).
"General Info." URL: http://www.ahepa.org/info/index.html.
Updated on May 26, 2004.

Hellenic Communication Service, L.L.C. "Kalos Oristate."
URL: http://www.helleniccomserve.com. Updated on May 26, 2004.

GoGreece.com. "Your Internet Guide to Greece."
URL: http://www.gogreece.com. Updated on May 26, 2004.

Preservation of American Hellenic History. "Home-page News."
URL: http://www.pahh.com. Updated on May 26, 2004.

Index